novum pro

Apollo Kikule

God's Solution To Man's Problems

St. Paul's Epistle To The Romans

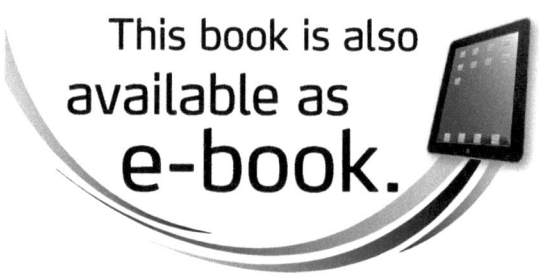

www.novum-publishing.co.uk

All rights of distribution, including via film, radio, and television, photomechanical reproduction, audio storage media, electronic data storage media, and the reprinting of portions of text, are reserved

Printed in the European Union on environmentally friendly, chlorine- and acid-free paper.

© 2016 novum publishing

ISBN 978-3-99048-566-8
Editing: Louise Darvid
Cover photo: Apollo Kikule
Cover design, layout & typesetting: novum publishing

www.novum-publishing.co.uk

PREFACE

Today Man reasons and rationalizes about many things: ways of alleviating poverty, war, disease, disasters, calamities, etc. but there is no answer coming forth. The darkened hearts have been made empty is God's just retribution.

Rationalizing gets us nowhere because man has traded God's glory (the Truth) for the perishable things of the world. Men reprobate God and hence His wrath (seen in the deteriorating condition of our world.)

In the Epistle to the Romans, we find God's answer to our problems in the world. It will not be the power of any super power or the most prosperous economy or the work of any visible Church to put matters right, or solve the problems of our world. Only God's utterance from the Scripture is the answer; and the Epistle to the Romans is one of the greatest spiritual weapons in man's hand to reverse the deteriorating condition of the world.

The Truth laid out in this Epistle forms the basis of a harmonious existence of human life on earth. Of course, the rest of God's utterances do the same, but the Epistle to the Romans is short yet comprehensive and is intended for our earthly existence. Obviously humanity has ignored all Scripture and God's answer to our rebellious existence is His wrath which appears in different forms as listed below:

1. Breakdown of the visible Church into different denominations for instead of being united by the Word we have the differing interpretations of the same. Surely these different interpretations cannot be right and the results of these are the many forms of worship which St. Paul strongly wrote against in this epistle and elsewhere.
2. Ever deteriorating abuse of fellow man from hatred in the heart of man, religious fanaticism which is the child birth of paganism, deteriorating family conditions, sectarianism, wars, unheard of strange behavior in all our society, young and old alike.
3. Natural disasters like floods, hunger, famine, poverty and the like in many parts of our world. These retributions, etc., are part of God's wrath for rebellious hearts.
4. But the worst of God's wrath is: the deprivation of the human mind of God's central control mechanisms – having no fear of God – a result of ungodliness in man's heart, the suppression of God's manifested Truth in His work of creation and Salvation.

It is for this reason that God Himself, the Author of life, once more gives us another opportunity to embrace Him; **the human writers like the Prophets and Apostles remain nothing more than just being mouthpieces** of God's utterances.

Here in the Epistle to the Romans, we find the Spiritual Solution in a nutshell which alone can reverse the current trend of our ungodliness. Ungodliness is the greatest sin. It is the original cause of God's condemnatory verdict of man's eternal death.

THE THEME IN THE EPISTLE TO THE ROMANS
God's Righteousness

1. **Romans Chapter 1:1-17 – God's Gospel**
    1. God's Gospel with its gift of righteousness
    2. The Son's Gospel – Obedience of faith
    3. God's gift of righteousness through faith

2. **Romans Chapter 1:18-32 – God's Wrath**
    1. Ungodliness (Sinfulness of man)
    2. Our Guilt thereof
    3. God's Revelation of His Wrath

3. **Romans Chapter 2: 1-29 – Moralism (Reliance on Law for Salvation)**
    1. Moralism (reliance on Law for reform or discipline)
    2. The Guilt thereof
    3. Moralism is the foe of the Gospel

4. **Romans Chapter 3:1-31 – The Advantage of the Gospel (The Word)**
    1. The Realization of Sin
    2. The Revelation of God's gift of Righteousness
    3. The Gospel is our Ransom

5. **Romans Chapter 4: 1-25 – The Gospel is the Sovereignty of God**
    1. Substitutes believers' faith for righteousness
    2. Establishes the spiritual quality
    3. Establishes the hope of our resurrection

6. **Romans Chapter 5: 1-21 –**
   God's Love is the fulfillment of the Law
   1. Our Deliverance – Christ's obedience.
   2. Our Redemption – the vicarious death
   3. Our Hope – The gift of the Holy Spirit

7. **Romans Chapter 6:1-23 –**
   The Gospel is Our Deliverance.
   1. Our Liberation – Baptism
   2. Faith Obedience – our enslavement to Righteousness
   3. Sanctification – the Spiritual body (Unity)

8. **Romans Chapter 7:1-25 –**
   The Gospel is our Redemption (or God's Law)
   1. Knowledge of Sin (Our Conversion)
   2. Deliverance from the law – (The Death of Christ)
   3. The glorious hope – (The New Spiritual Life)

9. **Romans Chapter 8:1-17 – The Gospel is our Spiritual Resurrection**
   1. The Law of the Spirit
   2. It is the fulfilled Promise that is Believers are fully redeemed – (evidence of spiritual life)
   3. The Law of the Spirit sanctifies

10. **Romans Chapter 8:18-39 –**
    Conforming to Christ's suffering
    1. God's loving providence (The called)
    2. God's purpose (conformity) – Repentance through the call
    3. Comfort – our actual confession and testimony

11. Romans Chapter 9:1-33 – God's Sovereignty and power.
　1. God's great plan of Salvation – the Seed of Israel
　2. Mercy for wretchedness
　3. Long Suffering (His patience with the vessels of wrath)

12. Romans Chapter 10:1-21 – The Supremacy of God
　1. One God, One Nation, One Rule of Righteousness
　2. His Lordship
　3. The utterance of faith

13. Romans Chapter 11: 1-36 – The Saving Purpose
　1. Election by Grace
　2. The Reconciliation of the World
　　(the marvel of divine grace)
　3. God's mercy – (not as one running or working)

14. Romans Chapter 12: 1-21 – Living Sacrifice
　1. The Portion of Faith – Our qualification and obligation
　2. The Doctrine – Our boundary
　3. Love – Our intelligence

**15. Romans Chapter 13: 1-14 –
God's Rule over the World – Authority**
　1. God's Authority
　2. God's Love
　3. God's Righteousness

**16. Romans Chapter 14:1-23 – The Intelligence –
(True Knowledge that attains purpose –
the Harmony in the Church)**
　1. Admonition
　2. Comprehension
　3. Purpose (distinction between law and grace)

17. Romans Chapter 15:1-33 – The Holy Spirit – (Power)
   1. Sanctification – (the unity – the believers' ability)
   2. Wisdom – (the ability to put each other in mind – the competency)
   3. Love – (the intelligence – the child birth of God's wisdom, the Christian bond – apostleship in case of Prophets, Apostles and all believers' Fellowship)

18. Romans Chapter 16:1-27 – God's Wisdom (Firmness of the Heart)
   1. Our Wisdom – (our great hope)
   2. Our Righteousness – (peace on earth)
   3. Our Sanctification – (Joy on earth)

ROMANS CHAPER 1:1-17
God's Gospel (With its gift of Righteousness)

The Christian congregation in Rome had distinctive characteristics and competences which were observable by all who came into contact with them. Ordinary people and travelers could see a membership having all different races, meeting together for worship without any disagreement within and without. Unity is the one distinguishing mark of the Gospel and such was this congregation in Rome. Jews, Gentiles, slaves from the imperial royalty, men and women plus children. All these met regularly as one congregation. Such was unheard of in the Jewish communities and Gentile World! This unity is what filled Paul's heart with inexplicable great joy. He heard of it in every city he travelled to in Asia; Macedonia, Achaia, Galatia etc. Paul and all disciples knew the underlying cause of this unity, namely – God's Gospel. The rest of the world could only see the distinctive characteristics of unity and of course did not understand the underlying causes.

It is this underlying feature of unity which Paul refers to as the faith being advertised all over the world. Not only had the pagan travelers talked about this congregation but the many Jewish travelers must have noted this outstanding competency. This congregation as a result was very different from the ever-striving, unsatisfiable populace in Rome. Conscious of God's power of grace (the effects of the Gospel) plus Paul's inner induced deep feeling and attraction towards all believers:

- Paul could not help but have an intense desire developed to visit this congregation whose spirit was of the same nature as his.
- Thus he introduced himself to this congregation in Rome by way of this Epistle as their own with one spiritual life marked by the obedience of faith which was kindled by God's Gospel.
- Which alone reveals God's Power of Grace – "His gift of Righteousness" Which is the greatest gift to mankind, and this alone unites all men as it did to this congregation in Rome.

God's Gospel consists of:
1) God's Gospel with its gift of righteousness
2) The Son's Gospel – the Obedience of Faith
3) God's gift of righteousness

1) God's Gospel with its gift of righteousness

God's Gospel deals with His Son. This is the whole written Word from Genesis to the last book of the New Testament i.e. the Book of Revelation. To interpret the term "Son" or (God's son) exhaustively, we should treat practically everything that is said in the entire Bible. God's son neither starts with the Birth of Jesus nor ends with His earthly career. It deals with His divine nature. God makes His own revelation of His Son, as having a divine nature from eternity to eternity and as such is the meaning of the Son. The two descriptions of the Son who is at the very heart of God's Gospel are:

i) The Promise
ii) The Fulfillment

The Promise and the Fulfillment consist of:
- His entrance into the state of **humiliation** for His saving work
- Then as the **Savior** – He entered His state of exaltation, a state in which He is in now.

Both rest on His existence as a Son from all eternity. These two states form the very heart of God's Gospel to the world in its apostleship.

a) His State of Humiliation – Grace (the saving power)

Thus He who is God became man without ceasing to be God, without change in His Deity, with no connotation of sin, but only that of limitation and weakness of our human nature. He came out of David's seed as the Messiah and thus all Messianic promises centered in Him pointing to the Kingly features in which He now rules in heaven, in full glory enthroned upon Him. The climax of which was His death on the Cross, He finished the Father's work on earth in His holy obedience and thus the Father glorified Him in power. This is God's power that saves man from sin and death – the very power of grace.

b) His glorified state (our confession – Lord) the confession by which we become slaves.

He was crowned with glory and honor (in power) because of His suffering and death (Hebrews 2:9) and these passages run throughout every Scripture statement regarding the two states of Christ. With these states we know the substance and contents of the Promised Gospel which Paul was commissioned to preach; namely;

"The Son's Name" which consists of both states of humiliation and exaltation (as Savior,) as it was confessed by all the slaves who bowed to it in the "obedience of faith" – The Name is "Our Lord."

The expression "Our Lord" contains the full confession and acknowledgment of God's Son, by this Lordship we refer to as the One – "who owns us" has purchased and won us. On whom all our trust and our obedience depend. This – His Holy obedience is what makes all believers slaves of Jesus Christ. Truly we are His property in the true sense of the word as indeed an earthly slave is owned by an earthly master – this ever then serves as a deem picture of our slavery to Our Lord Jesus Christ.

The term "Jesus" signifies the "Person," a reference to His Divine human nature during His humiliation, and "Christ" – a reference to His office; anointed our Prophet, High Priest and King all in one – in His saving capacity. This One is Paul's blessed Master under whom like Paul, all Romans and all believers have become slaves because He has paid the price of sin and death and thus saved us all including the Romans. Those who have no will of their own, except that of their Lord Christ who has saved them with His saving work, (Grace) with His sacrificial death.

c) **Apostleship – those with spiritual gift as witnesses of the author, owner and sender, with their obedience of faith.**

Over and above this wonderful Power of Grace by which we all become slaves of Christ, which also made Paul one of the slaves, there is another spiritual gift – favor, Grace that made Paul and the other twelve stand out more: as witnesses of the Power of God's Gospel "the humiliation and exaltation of God's Son to which Paul and the other Apostles were witnesses. As a result of this witness, Paul writes: "not as one being another slave of Christ but as an Apostle i.e. one who is called by Jesus Christ, a reference to an immediate call (i.e. a direct contact with Jesus Christ) – this made Paul one of the twelve. These twelve were set apart for "God's Gospel" meaning, as witnesses of the author, owner and sender.

They are witnesses of the authority of the Word as God's very own – as the Good News and the Apostles being the ones to whom the message was committed (whole heartedly dedicated.) This Good news was first committed to the Prophets in a form of advance promise. It was the very promise of God which the Prophets were chosen to convey – the message about the fulfillment to come. This fulfillment (the promised Salvation) was accomplished in Jesus Christ and these Apostles had to follow with the same identical Gospel message – same contents but now with the addition of the great fulfillment.

The Promises were conveyed in Words, we still have the words in writing – "in black and white" in the Holy Writings – a fully reliable medium for conveying His Promises to all men. And God enabled the Prophets and finally also the Apostles to transmit His words exactly as He wanted it transmitted. This is the verbal "inspiration" a simple fact. God speaks in and through these especially appointed men (Prophets and Apostles) and they reach back to Adam, and all exist for the Holy Promise – i.e. for Salvation – a reference to God's son who is "The Promise and Fulfillment" and this is what Paul refers to as the Grace and Apostleship.

The Apostleship (is this office) with its especially called bearers who are the Lord's gift to the entire Church plus the actual gift of Grace. This office – its main aim and purpose is for obedience of faith among all nations. It is this Apostleship which achieves Salvation.

The congregation in Rome had already received the Apostolic Gospel –the result of which was God's gift of righteousness through faith with its visible effect of unity which was advertised throughout the world to which Paul writes as an Apostle – with his heart drawn by the power and the same great desire and interest in extending the faith's obedience among all nations. This is the Son's Gospel.

2) The Son's Gospel – The Obedience of Faith

We have **God's Gospel** with the **Savior, our Lord as its content** and the **Apostleship** which transmits its power through the obedience of faith and both are known as Grace. All believers have received Grace and are thus called beloved or saints. The other name for this Grace is "*God's Love*" as constituting His Son. Love or Grace is a specific term referring to God's knowledge which is also God's son, which knowledge bestows the power of grace or Christ's righteousness through faith. The knowledge of God's Son with his obedience of faith filled Paul's heart with full fervor (intense and passionate feeling) for the Romans, though he had never met them. In the same manner this congregation was to feel exactly the same. When they received the apostolic letter, both Paul and the Romans felt real contact with each other's soul because they both received the great undeserved gift of grace.

The Effect of the power of grace – it draws believers together. See the contents of Paul's heart: you only need to look at the contents of the letter and how he reveals himself to them. This deep feeling is the result of a new life as a result of his connection with the Gospel and wished the Romans to have the same gift of the new life. It is the inner spiritual life and contact with God – that underlies all his apostolic work as it ought to underlie the work of all believers – "*I serve in my spirit*" in connection with the Gospel of His Son. This is Paul's personal worship in his own spirit in prayer. It is his personal spiritual connection with the Gospel of the Son – spiritual gift which draws all believers in one body.

Here the Son's Gospel enables Paul's spirit to draw near to God. You draw near to God by drawing near to His beloved people in a spiritual manner, by having the same knowledge of God's Gospel, resulting into a spiritual life which is expressed in confession, love and unity, which is the Son's Gospel with its power of grace. The purpose of spiritual drawing is to impart spiritual gifts to each other. For their confirmation: this is not a one sided act, it always has a mutual effect – upon him who imparts as upon him who receives. Thus for Paul to confirm others means something also for him, namely; jointly being comforted – with them. The confirming cannot be done without bringing about the other. This confirming is increase in the spiritual power which is ever manifested in confession, love and unity – all of which is subjective faith.

See the sequence and development of this power of God's love "faith." In Vs. 5, Paul united himself to the Romans by speaking of what "we" (the Romans and Paul) received (past) – the Gospel of God. But in Vs. 12, here he speaks of what he and the Romans jointly are to receive (future,) that is, being jointly comforted, encouraged, and cheered in a blessed, joint

experience, i.e. through each other's faith – both yours and mine in expectation of Paul's visit;
- This faith in its expression reveals itself by means of **confession, love and unity** or Salvation.
- It is true, that one of the happy experiences of Paul's ministry is this enjoyment of comfort which Paul looked forward to with such desire and it is sweeter because of the mutuality it involves;
- He prayed constantly to get to Rome, petitioned that God would soon shape His course to reality.
- Grace as a power makes us all believers; debtors of Grace. In case of Paul, to fulfill the official apostolic purpose to obtain some fruit of his apostolic labors in the great city before going to Spain – Rome was the center of the world.
- One nation but this obligation extended to other nations as well, the fruit is always faith which is kindled by the same power of grace.

The Gospel made him a debtor to both the educated and the uneducated, to all races – both Black and White in each nation. This he did not only in Ephesus but almost throughout all Asia in the region of Achaia and Macedonia. His apostleship made him the great debtor who could discharge his heavy obligation only in Gospel coin.

Preaching "the Gospel" is God's chosen strategy for "salvation" – through faith i.e. for all those believing to be saved. This strategy is what the world regards as "foolishness;" because they have chosen and preferred political systems governed by laws, pressure groups and the like, yet law is the very one for revealing sin and our condemnation through the law. The Gospel is what the whole world needs, the same preaching which makes wise the simple – the supreme requirement.

"Debtor" is the compulsion under which Paul worked – to obtain fruit – the fruit of believing souls through which God's righteousness is acquired and it is this righteousness which is to unify the world.

3) God's gift of Righteousness through faith

The great successful men of the world are found in big cities of this world – and that's where we all aspire to be, where we want to finish off our lives. These cities are the centers of power, glory, magnificence and riches and these are the earthly attractions which captivate all souls of men. One might draw the strongest contrast between these attractions and the Gospel.

The Gospel is no longer attractive and powerful as it was in Paul's day – man is no longer truly conscious of what the Gospel really is – all these earthly things have completely blindfolded man in such a manner that he has completely failed to see the destructive power of sin and hence our connection to the Creator and His verdict of death because of the ungodliness of the world. Sin and death is the one proof that all men are under the power of Satan, and are living in his kingdom of darkness – the earthly glory and attractions:

- Being completely blindfolded by the earthly attractions, man does not realize the source of his suffering and death there is in this world.
- All the suffering and death do not serve as signals of danger to man anymore and are meaningless to him and they

do not reveal that suffering and death are a result of sin which can be removed only by the Gospel.
- Man is living under the power of darkness yet he is not aware of God's adverse verdict of eternal death nor does he realize God's gracious gift of grace which alone removes his sinful condition through faith in God's Gospel. It is thus we say the World belongs to the devil. And the world with all its attractions offers no credible solution to save mankind. The Gospel is God's power of – His righteousness through faith alone which saves mankind from Sin and death.
- To reject the Gospel is thus to reject being saved from eternal death.
- It is to desire death more than life everlasting.
- It is to be blinded by the earthly lures more than the Gospel righteousness.
- In the things of the world, its power, glory and magnificence, there is no power even to save one little bit.
- The Gospel snatches sinners away from Satan's kingdom of darkness and doom by the gift of God's righteousness through faith.
- This is the view of the Son's Gospel that must shine out gloriously, draw and attract us so that we too may be saved.

How does this Son's Gospel save?
The Gospel saves when preached, when it comes into contact with us and when it kindles faith i.e. when one puts his entire trust in what it offers. It is the very nature of the Gospel to make him who hears it a "believer" – thereby saving him. We need to understand well what the Gospel is, namely; it is not only the Truth and Divine reality – it is the most blessed Truth in the Universe – the most personal truth for every sin-

ner which reaches into the soul in order to save man from the curse and the doom of his sin, by making you and me God's own through faith in Jesus Christ.

The truth above all truth is the Divine saving truth which includes faith, confidence and trust. Woe unto him who rejects this truth and trusts the lie! Being saved is simple (easy to understand) by working confidence in the heart, the Gospel bestows God's righteousness.

Faith is the one door to Salvation – by getting into contact with the Gospel, the heart becomes enlightened then assured and finally confident – all of which constitute God's righteousness and in this manner the Gospel saves.

This righteousness is justification by faith alone
In fact, both God's wrath and His Righteousness are revealed in this Gospel.
- The one (the wrath) is in law which condemns – and the other the Gospel that saves. God's righteousness had to be revealed otherwise none of us would know anything about it.
- For the only righteousness which man can think of is man's own self-made righteousness.

The Righteousness of God is entirely an attribute of God. God only bestows the status of His righteous verdict to those who have believed. This status of righteousness never springs from any works of ours, nor does it spring from any good moral behavior – it is God's verdict of righteousness upon a sinner. On the basis of this personal justification is Christ's blood and righteousness which became effective the day He died and rose again.

It was the happiest day of Luther's life when he discovered that "God's Righteousness" as used in the Epistle to the

Romans means God's verdict of righteousness upon a believer. This joy is ours today – to all believers – a status of righteousness into which faith and the believer are placed by God's verdict of righteousness.

This is the doctrine of justification by faith alone and this is the sum of God's Gospel. This righteousness is the power of grace which the Gospel offers as a gift to everyone who believes. This is God's Righteousness out of faith unto faith. Revealing takes place in the preached Gospel in connection with the saving power of the preached Gospel which is so efficient in creating faith in the heart. Man is ever inclined to discount faith, to elevate something else, but God centers everything in the faith he creates by the Gospel righteousness.

This first part of the chapter reveals a summary of God's Gospel of grace with its righteousness. The next part of the chapter reveals man's sinfulness with its wrath which the Law reveals. The Law is God's medium to reveal the sinfulness of man (the ungodliness) for which all humanity was condemned to death.

ROMANS CHAPTER 1: 18-32
God's Wrath

We should not wonder at the ever deteriorating conditions of this world. The Scripture is very clear about the cause of these bad things because the world has rejected God's divine existence and governance. It does not recognize God as the author and creator of the universe. Man should have appreciated God's providences; the fruit of the earth in its seasons, the wisdom and understanding of men with which they have utilized the earthly resources to their greatest advantage, then the abilities of our bodies, the mind, the strength and thoughtfulness of man. These, man takes for granted! He never asks himself where they come from and who is in control of all these. **God answers all this ungratefulness with the constant retributions which are visited to all creation and so we have natural disasters, hatred, thieves, wars, hunger, deprivation and finally eternal death visited to all mankind and all creation because of the sin of ungodliness in men** – which is the rejection of God's divine existence and governance.

All these retributions do not happen by chance but it is God's very means by which He reveals himself to man but continuously being ignored and rejected. In the place of this revelation, man places his own theories like evolution and the like.

God's answer to this rejection is the revelation of His wrath which Paul unfolds in this second half of Romans Chapter One. Suppressing the quantum knowledge of all God's providences results in His constant retributions because the hearts of men do not know God hence he sends his wrath including eternal death.

So we need to understand what ungodliness or the sin of man really means as presented here:
1) Ungodliness (sinfulness of man)
2) Our Guilt thereof
3) God's Revelation of His Wrath

1) Ungodliness (Sinfulness of Man)

Man's greatest sin in the sight of God is this ungodliness which results into unrighteousness. In this activity of ungodliness man's heart suppresses all the truth there is in this world, from exerting its power in the heart and life. God has made two outstanding revelations:
i) The type of righteousness He requires – which is revealed in the Gospel as detailed out in Verses 1–17.
ii) His wrath towards man which does not need a medium like that of the Gospel. Yet God makes this wrath so clear and distinct to all men by visiting it to us every now and then. God's truth which men suppress includes the following;
- The whole work of creation
- The countless beneficent providences
- The ever renewed retributions by man's own mind, especially his moral nature and his conscience

This whole knowledge of creation God has made manifest so clearly in order that we should seek Him, feel after Him and ultimately find Him. How does this knowledge of creation make God manifest or make clearly visible to our eyes and

understanding? These visible things of God's creation should reveal to man's mind the invisible things regarding God. This whole knowledge is a unit;
- Clearly seeing the unseen things is a mental act, one which is not abstract speculation but sane and sober thought of the things made by God, all of which advertise His existence, power and divinity. It is a mental act yet one that does not exclude sense – perception.
- All men (from the beginning of the world) who have ever lived have had a great revelation concerning God.
- Man's mind should reflect on "the things God made." We have all had a long time to do it – like all others. Paul makes a startling conclusion which reveals all that the mind of the human race has contemplated (has examined, observed and scrutinized) of the things God made.

Visible things
- All of them proclaim the continuity of day and night.
- Providences year after year from God. And so David's heart sang constantly:
"*The Heavens declare the glory of God and the firmament sheweth His Handiwork.*"
"*Day unto day uttereth speech and night unto night sheweth knowledge. There is no speech nor language where their voice is not heard.*"
(Psalms 19:1–3)

Our Perception
- We see these things – and then by use of our perception – we can then say: yes we see; that behind the world of created things, there is a power that never grows old or infirm or fades out.

- This is the power of God's Omnipotence – His everlasting Power.
- Not only that quality, but also others such as His knowledge, wisdom, goodness, kindness, justice etc. – all that His great creation reflects and much more: which are all His Divine nature – His attributes.
- Then the other things we see by perception of our minds through our natural eyes: whatever power exists in any creature is bound to fade and die out i.e. the created world must and will come to an end; and this should lead to **one conclusion**:
- God's created things convey more to us than their own undeniable existence, having a mind by mental perception we see the invisible God, His **Omnipotence, Divinity** and **Power**.

This is natural theology, which is universal in scope and does not need a special medium like the Gospel. However the Scriptures record natural theology in many places, Acts 17:24–29 is just one of them.

What does man do with this theology? Paul tells us; men rendered it ineffective and we too have done the same. How? Paul tells us: "man suppresses the manifested truth." This truth should have been made the fundamental basis of man's heart and its principle should be God. This should be the beginning of every man to search and find God. God is not only the proper basis of reasoning thus leading to the fundamental essential ground of every heart or rule of behavior in the interest not only of the society but also for the true life which does not end here but in eternity.

The moment this truth is allowed to control man, ungodliness is cast out and thus godliness enters. It is thus God makes this truth so clear, distinct to all men. Men cannot accuse God of hiding Himself from them and thus excuse their irreligion, misinterpretations and their immorality. His whole work of creation is the truth by which man suppresses and there by rejects God. Yet He made it so clear to men so that man may seek God, feel after Him and find Him.

- In their rejection they go counter to this mass of truth regarding God.
- This is where unbelief springs from and this unbelief is the rejection of the right norm and principle of our hearts and of our lives and this results in *the sin* of man or ungodliness and unrighteousness.

The heart which does not know God results in having all types of different gods hence ungodliness which results in "unrighteousness" or the immorality in the world. Paul further proceeds to provide the proof that man is guilty ungodliness and reveals the immorality of the world.

2) Our Guilt thereof

What have we done so far with our knowledge of truth? Although we know God (as the Jews knew Him) i.e. realized His everlasting power and divinity: they did not let this knowledge control or even check them. They refused to treat Him as God and give Him thanks. **Glorifying God occurs when men recognize who and what He is and act accordingly** i.e. embrace Christ, worship, honor, praise and serve Him. They did not glorify God hence they could not give thanks.

To glorify God is to think of Him alone and thank Him for what we have received from Him. The second is less than the first; to think of God's benefactions when giving thanks is more: to thank Him at least because of gratefulness is less. The result of the refusal to do the two: i.e. the refusal to glorify and to give thanks is the reason why men became empty in their reasoning which led to senseless hearts which became darkened.

So Paul states: they were made empty – their hearts were darkened by God in His just retribution. It is due to man's refusal to glorify and thank God that He has caused men and the world over to get into this *pitiful state.* This pitiful state is observable everywhere you go.

- Today men reason and reason about God, men of old did the same. Every man has his own rationalization about God but all this thinking about God is utterly useless – it leads to nothing; gets to no real goal.
- Instead of arriving at God, it only thinks it arrives and ends by denying God. Thus men in their reasoning become empty.
- Men ought to have known God because through the created world God obtrudes Himself in His wrath.
- Yes, they keep reasoning and rationalizing but they get nowhere because of the wrath from Him. They refuse to do either because of their immorality – Verse 18, i.e. a heart that does not know God which is their immorality – their determination not to let God's norm of right rule them and their lives.
- They suppress the truth with their unrighteousness and thus despite all their reasoning they end up in emptiness.
- So also "their senseless hearts become darkened" completely so – because their hearts have no comprehension and understanding. In a word, they become darkened.

- Light indeed abounds (exists in large amounts) all nature radiates it and seeks to illuminate the heart, but this senseless heart sees and yet does not see, knows and yet does not know.

And worse still:
- Claiming to be wise, they become foolish.
- Reasoning that gets man nowhere is truly foolishness.
- A senseless heart that even prides itself because of such reasoning is utterly foolish, becomes silly as one who shows a lack of common sense or judgment.

It has always been the boast of the ungodly and the unrighteous that they are "wise" in their thinking, reason and so forth. They look down upon believers for their faith in God and in Christ.

"Silly" is Paul's verdict – just plain silly!

Any heart without God's whole knowledge of creation results into unrighteousness which is the refusal to bow to what all creation proclaims concerning God; and thus it is silly.

This silliness advances much further to a climax.

How outstandingly foolish men become when they boast about being wise: they actually exchange (or trade) the glory of the incorruptible God for an image – likeness of corruptible man and even lower – yes – the lowest creatures. Can folly (foolishness) go further? Paul names the extreme – all the lesser are included. Only a fool would trade the glorious incorruption for fiction that is empty and worse than empty, namely; false and degrading.

The glory of God is the sum of His attributes as these constitute His essence, the sum of the perfections of His Being – but as shining forth to us and revealing what God is for us.

The glory of God is infinitely blessed for man – for this glory is life eternal *"that they might know Thee, the only True God and Jesus Christ whom Thou hast sent." (John 17:3.)*

The "incorruptible" God, imperishable in His Being and His attributes in contrast with "corruptible" man and lower creatures, this contrast brings out the full desperate folly of exchange.

- Men have given up the infinite, imperishable fountain of blessing which God intended for them by their true knowledge of Him whom they have traded for even less than a corruptible man, from whom they might hope for a little, at least for a few years, for only an image – likeness of a corruptible man, from which they derive absolutely nothing, for such a likeness of brute creatures, including the lowest that crawl, heroes, kings, celebrities, games, entertainment etc. This is the guilt of man, we see the terrible exchange; corruptible instead of incorruptible. Guilty indeed is man in his emptiness.

3) God's Revelation of His Wrath

What is God's answer to this terrible exchange?
- To all this unrighteousness – when God is thrown out of the heart – men probate God. God's answer is the divine punishment for their rejection of Him – so God gave them over. Paul presents three great features of this righteous judgment; three terrible sides of judgment: the worst sin into which their ungodliness plunged them.

a) **The principle (godliness) is thrown out** – uncleanliness enters (senseless)

God's action is judicial – when God is completely cast off, when the measure of ungodliness overflows, His punitive justice hands the sinners over completely to their sins in order to let sin run into excess and destroy the sinner.

Thus God uses sin to punish itself and the sinners. It is the desire for all men to get as much honor as possible especially also to make their bodies as grand as possible, as beautiful as possible – but to look closely at them;

- They wallow in the uncleanliness of moral filth – they disgrace themselves – see all these superstars – these are the wise, who are fools. Yes indeed they must live the life, they must be free of all restraints, they must get drunk with every pleasure – but their bodies pay for it in the end. The root of sin and its judgment is "ungodliness," the blessed God no longer controls these men, hence they wreck their lives.
- They have traded for the lie: idols and image likeness: a very frightful trade indeed. The worship of creatures such as the World Cup more than the Creator. They have venerated the created things – the unclean things. Their desires grow into passions which grow bitter and even end in death.
- Vile practices which go beyond normal relations; Paul gives only a sample, and for these aberrations men receive duly the inescapable recompense.
- Then these vile practices result into the basest sensuality and multitudes of other vices.
- Men probate God!!!

b) Basest sensuality

By abandoning the knowledge of God, He gave them over to the sin they would not let go of at any price.

- To the most disgraceful and disgusting forms, and their delusion in practicing these, they receive as due reward the awful results in their own corroding bodies. Examples: many human experiences, sexual sins – newspapers record their constant devastation. The moment God is taken out of the center of man's life – the stench of sex aberration is bound to rise – it is so true the world over to this day without God; sex runs wild.
- The alarmed (the Church, government bodies, international organizations etc.) constantly debate what can be done to check the worst damage; impotent reformers set up their little dams (Law) – only to see them swept away.
- Legislation and the courts can do nothing.
- There is only one hope; putting the real fear of God into the heart of man.

Our modern educators rather destroy the fear of God which means the world is ripening for its doom.

From sensuality to a probate mind, every taste would discard God. So many of the wise fools are proud, when their grasp of mind threw out God. Once the principle is thrown out – the wrath is intensified; man's heart is filled with viciousness – intentionally harmful or nasty. Here we see men full of envy, murder, strife, cunningness which today is referred to with many bad descriptions without the principle; they all blossom out of a heart that has thrown out God – wickedness.

c) Active wickedness or viciousness (faithless)
Sadly; when God is thrown out we get God haters, then men who spread evil about others.
- When men hate God with insolence, they insult and inflict others with injury. They are hateful to God on this account.
- Arrogant boasters – who lift themselves above others.
- Base men intending only to hurt others.

Beginning life viciously, the young are bound to go on in life in a vicious way. The present cry is the lack of parental control, the rebelliousness of the youth (merciless children.) Godless parents raise godless children and thus get to taste the bitter fruits of their own sowing in their offspring. The fear of God is the true source of filial (devoted, respectful) obedience. The fruits of wickedness from their parents spirals on.

The result of all the above is a senseless, faithless, loveless and merciless society – with vicious youth.

A senseless heart – a terrible indictment to "lack sense," the ability to put two and two together in the moral life.

Faithless society – false to covenants, agreements – even in their strongest promises, their own word cannot be trusted.

Loveless – in the sense of common natural human affection yet even brutes show love, examples of lovelessness abound: patricide, matricide, fratricide.

One father can take care of ten children, but the ten children are unable to care for one father (or mother). Alas!

Today we see that even the natural affection has wilted – is dying – is dead already where nature itself leads us to expect it. The more godless, the more merciless – might is right. Paganism manifests all these vices: what Judaism was capable of – its treatment of Jesus, the Apostles and the Christians. Even today nothing is too low, too outrageous to stoop to attain its end. **We live in a society where we all see the wrong increasing: no one knows which turn to expect in the future. This is God's own manifestation of His wrath because men have abandoned the principle which controls the heart and hence God's own retribution. Let their own sin do the job of punishing this ungodliness.**

In this last part of Chapter One, Paul perfectly presents God's answer to a world which has rejected its principle of control.

ROMANS CHAPTER 2:1-29
MORALISM - (the Reliance on law for Salvation and governance)

Man's inability to use and apply law as the means of governance, from the observable evidence – has left the entire world and individual countries sinking deeper and deeper into chaos. Law is like a bridle of the horse; it can only constrain but cannot control or tame the heart of man. Law is not the means God ordained to correct and remove the sinfulness of man, which is responsible for all the chaos and ultimately eternal death. Sin – which is any action or omission which constitutes an offense or crime starts in the heart of man long after any Law is in place, and consequently being broken. The world leaders and many religious leaders have refused to accept the fact that all the evil there is in this world cannot be cured by law and it will never be, so the chaos will continue to increase and many religions will continue to preach reform through law until the last man is wiped out off the face of the earth.

    The belief that law works to affect good behavior is the delusion of man. Law can only give rise to particular systems or principles distinguishing between right and wrong, good or bad behavior which is known as the moralism of men, and this cannot change people's heart. Over and against moralism is God's own ordained means of correcting bad behavior and thereby living peacefully in this world – by the use of God's uttered Word – the Gospel which consists of God's Council or the rule of grace. The evils of moralism are revealed by God's own law to the highest degree. In this chapter Paul reveals moralism as the greatest foe of the Gospel. The world is guilty of moralism hence the deteriorating conditions. You find one group accuses another of the wrongs without seeing the planks in their own eyes.

So this chapter reveals to us; the evils of relying on law.
1) Moralism (reliance on law for reform or discipline of society)
2) The Guilt thereof
3) Constituting the foe of the Gospel

1) Moralism – Delusion of Man

The source of sin in man is the rejection of God as the Creator of the world, Author and Giver of Life. This knowledge should have compelled man to seek and find God, and be controlled by Him alone with His Divine power. Man has rejected this knowledge which should control him through the Scriptures and this is the prime source of sin. God's verdict: guilty and eternal death. Law or any other system of law therefore cannot be used to reverse this trend and its use can only give rise to moralism, no matter what law exerts.

This rejection of God as the creator is the ungodliness of the world which gives rise to unrighteousness (i.e. having different gods in the heart) – and therefore turning to the use of law as the means of reform can only lead to fatuous moralism, in short – chaotic behavior.

Many Church leaders who are supposed to use and rely on the Divine power of the Gospel, have fallen into the same delusion of using law – even such law as that of Mosaic written law.

The worst feature of moralism is that it assumes a judgmental role – so a preacher of law by implication must stand in the judgment seat. A moralist wants reform by adopting the laws laid down. The Inspired Word of God tells us here that any man who judges and preaches reform through law, is the worst criminal to be thrust into the inner prison, where only the worst criminals are confined because: all humanity is already locked up into this inner prison of ungodliness and unrighteousness – so are all those who preach reform and set themselves as guides for others, who ask men to stop breaking the Law. Such a preacher is a prisoner blaming other prisoners for the same crime – this is the greatest hypocrisy in this world. Moralism assumes the preacher or judge has reformed, that he is holy and so he commands others to obey every law – but see the evils against him;

1) Many of the moralistic preachers are honorable people in the sight of men, they keep clear of the grosser forms of sin, but what about those sins in view of Matthew 15:19 such as evil thoughts, such as adultery, fornication, false witness, etc.? All of us are prisoners of this scourge of the evil mind; we are all ungodly and thus guilty, so none of us can preach to anyone about upholding the Law, for we are all sinners after having transgressed the Law first through Adam.

2) Any person applying law can only judge the outside but not the inside of the heart. In fact it is in most cases a matter of hiring a most dramatic lawyer and the criminal will walk away innocent even though guilty and deserving the death penalty. Many criminals have walked out free while many innocent people have faced death.

3) Even our Lord who can judge the inside of the heart does not condemn those who are penitent (John 8:15–16) and His judgment is one with the Father – good and valid in heavenly courts.

4) It is not the business of man to judge or preach reform through law to other persons, no matter how sinful. This is because law can neither change the heart of man, nor give him the true capacity to judge aright – for we cannot see the inside of the heart of man – it is only God who is the righteous judge because he alone can see the inside of man and judges him aright.

Many criminal leaders walk free from all charges simply by crossing borders, but does this clear the heart of their transgression of law? Of course not. But this was the case with the woman caught in adultery – she was let free simply because Jesus saw that all the men who were accusing her were sinners themselves – (John 8:15–16), this is in fact the purpose of the law – **to reveal to all of us, without exception, that we are sinners**. Does this mean that we should scrap all legal institutions, courts, laws of the land and the like? The restraints of law are required by those who are not believers but for those who are in Christ, He is Law unto them who love Him – for in Him God's law is fulfilled. For the way of peace they (the moralists) have not known – (Romans 3:17).

Moralists put their followers into a delusive security for they too are awaiting the final judgment from God on the last day, no matter what earthly verdicts they pronounce to both the criminal and the innocent. The moralists and his followers remain guilty of sin.

Moralists such as many of our judges, some Church leaders of our day – and indeed many men in high offices of our day – these are greatly rewarded and justifiably so because of the heavy load of judging between right and wrong: but in this way they are counting themselves secure or compliant hence misconceive God's beneficence towards them.

- God's favor of all earthly blessings is mistakenly taken to be God's approval of the moralist – the whole activity of reforming through law – this falsity is a very frightful thing.

God's goodness to all sinners – all men including the moralist – law is intended to lead all men to true repentance. Surely God's blessing cannot be an end in itself, it must have an ulterior end or purpose, something greater and final.
- Yes the beast can fill its belly from day to day and then come to an end, but not so with man.
- Here we see the statement of purpose in the world of sinners including the moralists, all are aimed at repentance, so that when God comes with His Gospel, men may bow in contrition and faith – (Acts 17:30).

What is God's answer to the moralism of this world?

Here we need to understand the implication of moralism: Men refer to it as the leading power of reform in God's created world thus defiling God's house.
- God's answer to moralism – is His wrath – i.e. the ever deteriorating conditions of the world and this trend will not abate.
- Any reform through law makes the heart hard and obstructs true repentance and only heaps up wrath. The final day will clear up many questions.

Moralism is the greatest foe of the Gospel, for it pretends to be the way of escape from judgment of God on all godlessness and wickedness of man, yet it only plunges man into deeper guilt. Moralism must be destroyed in order for the Gospel to stand. Moralism does not support the Gospel, in fact it opposes the Gospel.

2) The Guilt of man - as evidenced by his conscience

Law in general consists of the written and unwritten law. The earliest records of man's written code of law are: the Jewish laws i.e. the Law of Moses, the Greek ethics and in particular, the Roman law which has actually found its way into the modern world. Law is any system of rules regulating the actions and omissions of men and such a system is enforced by the imposition of penalties. Law may be written; i.e. created by legislation as distinguished from unwritten or common law, which is mainly derived and observed from customs and behavior of human beings.

What man must admit is the fact that these things of law are also found among the hearts of the uneducated, the pagan - who have never heard of such written laws, and this is the conscience of man which makes all men feel guilty of any breach.

- The conscience of man consists of the first table of the Law referred to in the Scriptures.
- It is thus we find that even the pagans and the uneducated comply with the things of the written law in their hearts.
- This work of the Law is largely found among the pagan and uneducated while it is noticeably missing among the educated.
- Law written in our hearts is also referred to as the image of God still left in our hearts after the fall of man. This is what man ordinarily refers to as the moral sense (ability to distinguish between right and wrong) or the conscience of man.

The entire activity of a conscience is nothing **but testimony of all actions of man** - in both the pagan as well as the

Christian. For example: on the things the conscience considers wrong: these reasonings, many band together in making accusations inside our hearts (most of the time;) and sometimes, not so often, the conscience judges or considers something we have done right and then "offers defense" in supporting those actions. For a bad thing, you may hash the conscience and if you do – still conscience goes against you. It literally bands together to batter down the victim, but when a man is blamed by other men, because of the conscience one after another stand by him.

Why then is this conscience in every man?

What the conscience of man attests is in connection with the final day when men's full accountability and conviction – guilt, will all be revealed;

- Nothing will be hidden.
- God will probe even the hidden things of men.
- And our individual conscience will be the evidence of the truth men suppress; His Power and Divinity, the truth we have hashed out of our conscience – revealing our disobedience. Our hearts will show we have rejected God as the Author of life and of the world. Cancel this day or hash up the conscience and the keystone in this life is broken out of the arch of all moral systems in the entire world.

Moral reasonings or conscience will have no purpose then – no aim – we can as well be like the wild beasts, without moral responsibility, all moral impetus to do things of the law gone except to eat and procreate.

- Conscience will convict each one of us in the acts we have done which have been against it.
- Conscience will reveal our ungodliness and the refusal to accept Him (God) as the one who is overall – the Creator.

- It will reveal our attempts to escape by our own means such as moralistic works.
- It will reveal our being against the Truth (reliance on the law instead of the Gospel).
- So conscience will make all of us guilty on that day of final judgment.
- No man will escape this condemnation by our own individual consciences.

What worries even the pagan when he condemns himself in the court of conscience is the higher court of God with its judgment on that day to come. The power of the conscience lies also in this, that no man shall exempt himself from God's final judgment. All men shall stand exposed before God's throne with their secret thoughts on that day, the guilt or testimony of our conscience will go against all moralistic behavior. It is our individual consciences which will present us as guilty before God, the supreme judge, on that day.

3) Moralism blinds man – The foe of the Gospel

God's original plan for man is salvation – i.e. eternal life. This life eternal comes not from mere knowledge of right or wrong, good or wicked deeds, but from testing God's essentials which is the acceptance of the Gospel as the only means of escape from God's wrath. What God's Gospel asserts is the fact that moralism or governance by law misguides man by acting as the great guide for others;

- That men are so blinded by moralism that they fail to taste the Gospel, thus they fail to see the essentials and never apply the essentials of the Law to themselves.

Any man who preaches law (moralist) as the means of reform is thus the greatest enemy of God's Gospel. Unfortunately these are the majority today. Pronouncements are made against some sinners while forgetting that they too (those making the pronouncements) are locked up in the same prison of criminals worthy of eternal death.

What then are God's essentials? God's essential for salvation consists of; the Gospel.

It is Law (especially the first table) which in the first place connects us to God by producing the guilt of sin in our conscience and our being worthy of death.

- The guilt of a conscience produced by the effect of law and the fright of death, should send every man to search for God.
- This search (like the Ethiopian eunuch) God rewards by revealing His own will i.e. the gift of salvation (the Gospel.) This is the proper testing of the essentials. But the moralist who acts as a teacher, i.e. guiding men from darkness to light – in V20 the educator of men, does not act on full knowledge of the law. What he uses is only part of the truth, i.e. law in general – which is a big mistake.
- Law which is supposed to produce the guilt, he uses as a reform tool – this is the wrong testing. The results of the Scriptures give proof which leaves this moralist completely destroyed by use of assumptions.
- If thou as one teaching another, don't you teach yourself not to steal; adultery, covetousness, etc.? The three that even the casuist must condemn.

- It is morally axiomatic (self-evident and unquestionable) that a teacher must first teach himself especially in matters of religion.

In this manner, the moralistic teachers condemn themselves and so did the Jewish moralists of Paul's day. The congregation in Rome must not succumb to this obnoxious disease of moralism i.e. "they sat as teachers in Moses' seat and yet they say but do not themselves." (Matthew 23:1-3)

This is the constant flow of moralism, they tell others to do but they do not themselves. This is the record of many of our churches today (not all) but in many cases worse than those of Paul's day. The embezzlements and various immoralities are voiced – Paul asks if moralistic teaching was truthful, don't they teach themselves first?

Let us not be deceived on this point; moralism cannot change the heart of man – even the moralist himself despite all his teaching of others, he leaves his own heart untaught and does no better than others. Many might say no, no, no! This is impossible! It cannot happen. Jesus Himself openly charged against these very Jewish moralists: "devouring widows' houses." (Matthew 23:14)

Moralism is powerless to free the moralist's own heart from covetousness and greed and thus in any number of ways appropriating what does not belong to him; and yet they will continue their moral preachments. Here with this exposure, all the moralists' lips will remain sealed and will offer no denial to these assumptions;

- Which one of us does not succumb to the evil thought of our minds?
- How about our own lasciviousness such as the fleshy carnal desires?

- How about our drive for riches, a better house, a new car, a new suit – covetousness.

How then can any one of us ever stand on a platform to preach reform through the law? This indeed is the greatest contradiction in mankind.

The moralist *"glorifies"* himself in the law but *"dishonors"* God through transgression of the law – the inescapable references from the long list of conditions already laid down. In this manner the Name – (the Gospel) which is supposed to be the door to salvation is blasphemed through what men receive from moralistic preaching.

In Israel Judaism had religious leaders who were most admired and followed by the great body of the nation – these were moralists and among them were the Scribes, Pharisees and the Rabbis. These leaders had to be overthrown to pave the way for the true Gospel, and so must most of religious leaders today.

The greatest law in Judaism was that of circumcision and many Jews used to brag as having done this act – and in their bragging as such, their hearts were uncircumcised as Paul says. In the end they rejected the Gospel – the very Author of life and even put Him to death thus they rejected the essentials.

The Gentiles had no such a mark, no such a heart that would murder an innocent person – shall not foreskin judge thee? – was Paul's deadly destruction of the moralist.

Many pagans (men in the sense of non-believers) do more things of the Law than the Christian moralists; won't these judge thee in God's Divine court of justice?

When Paul uses "Law" without the article "the" he refers to Law in general, but with the article "the Law" it is in reference to the whole Gospel with the great seal of salvation, through the "obedience of faith" and not merely mosaic code, the annulment of that seal i.e. the Jewish disobedience to "the Law."

Therefore men with circumcised hearts and spirits mean they believed the Old Testament Gospel – thus were justified and are righteous – God's good law produced the sinful condition in their hearts which compelled them to embrace the Gospel through the obedience of faith.

ROMANS CHAPTER 3:1-31
The Advantage of the Gospel (The Word)

All men are sinners we live in this earthly life without ever realizing our sinful condition. Sinfulness does not occur as a result of breaking any law but from lack of understanding the purpose of the created world, which is intended to make man seek God and find Him. Unfortunately no man cares who really the Creator is. The rebelliousness of human beings for not seeking after the Creator – is the greatest sin of the world known as godlessness – resulting into all different forms of worship. Each one having his own form of worship – this is the sinfulness of the world. Hearts that cannot think about the true God – hearts that can only think of entertainment, leisure, riches, friendships, preferred individual preachers with their styles etc. This is the godlessness to which God visits His wrath from the beginning of the world to the end – which climaxes in eternal death. (How could we ever arrive at this knowledge of our sinfulness without the Word?) How on earth would we ever have known about this fallen state of man or our ungodliness? How are we ever to be lifted out of our sinfulness and godlessness? Here is the great advantage we have in the Word consisting of the following:
1) The Realization of sin
2) The Revelation of God's righteousness
3) Our Ransom

1) The Realization of Sin

"The Law" is the Jewish name for the first five books of Moses and those of the Prophets. It is also the entire Old Testament (the Law and the Prophets). "The Law" is different from "Law" in general – which is the dos and don'ts. Law in general is not something to aid us reach God's demands but a mark of failure or the fallenness of man. It is "the Law" such as the Gospel in which **we have this great advantage of sin realization. In "the Law" we have the great advantage of the knowledge of sin, the depravity of man** – human failure to respond to the divine power. The Law is the Gospel of Christ with His mission which reveals sin in its totality especially with His death.

Godless are the hearts of all men and the proof is Romans 1:18–32. Now Paul goes further to provide Scriptural proof that even us who say we are Christians are included – the proof that shuts every mouth. The Scripture stops every mouth. Many Christians think that when they become saved they cease to be sinners – here Paul provides the "fallen human condition" including believers as well, from birth to the end of life on earth. The universal condition of Sin from Isaiah and Romans 3:10–18 states that not one doing good – meaning – not one is righteous. God looked down from Heaven to see.

The deadly sinful life is here pictured by the mouth as an opened sepulcher as the metaphor of an opened tomb – it is the very one that kills. **This mouth is full of deceit that kills by deceit and by the deceit of the tongue it gets its victim**. The desire to kill starts from the heart. A heart that is godless only continues to kill.

Those deceived suffer full curse and bitterness (Psalms 10:7), fraud – i.e. struck down with a curse and are victims of bitter fraud. In their path there is found ruthlessness, devastating feet crushing and shattering, leaving trails of misery to tell where they have been like a tornado storm. History is full of broad bloody trails and countless cruelties as miniature copies. It is the purpose of the Law to reveal sinfulness which is all a result of ungodliness. The heart is the very source of sin because there is no fear of God before their eyes – the source of all primal sinfulness because they did not know God.

The Law does a great service to humanity; they are God's spoken statements and proof about sinfulness of lives: It is not only Law such as that of the Mosaic code or any written law that reveals sin but the whole scripture or the Gospel.

- The Law deals with sinners only.

If there was no Gospel we should have no revealed Sin. The Law and the Gospel meet in the great fact of universal sin. The Old Testament is full of Law and Gospel so also is the New Testament. Both Law and the Gospel deal with sin – the one shows its guilt and penalty, the other shows its removal and thus the both together produce contrition and faith in the heart. In every part of Christ's suffering we see our sin. So both the Old and the New Testament speak to all who have it and stop every mouth and indeed the entire world becomes subject to condemnation and thus eternal death.

- This entire sum of the Scriptures is Sin and its removal all of which is picked up from various places; and we should note that not one of them is taken from the Mosaic code, not one is taken from the writings of Moses, the Pentateuch.
- They are quoted from Psalms and from Isaiah.
- And these Paul treats as being representative of the Law or the Scriptures.

With the Law – every mouth is stopped i.e. silenced by the indictment of being absolutely guilty and unable to make even the least defense. The whole world collectively – the Judge looks at every individual and then at the whole mass. First the silence of the accused, then the verdict upon one and all: become subject to punishment from God. If every mouth is stopped – here is the tragedy of today's moralistic teaching; reforming by adhering to Law (in general) – even such Law as that of the Mosaic code – the very one which convicts us, indeed stops every mouth, not a single mortal flesh will ever win acquittal through reform by adhering to Law, whose purpose is only to reveal sin. Law which included not only that of Moses, but any and every ethical code; serves one major purpose only – there comes only sin's realization.

Sin is more than just mere knowledge of missing the mark; it is "full realization" borne upon, the personal inner conviction of our own sin – hence Law reveals what sin does and so makes us realize what sin is. Law is the medium for sin. God's Word is the very means of revealing sin – a wonderful advantage we have in God's Word. Here in the Word we come to realize our sinfulness – the very conviction forever abolishes all moralistic delusions that after all we sinners might be justified because of works of law that in some way are wrought by ourselves.

- Law only produces the realization (conviction) of sin.

2) The Revelation of God's gift of Righteousness

"Righteousness" in earthly terms refers to: conforming to the acceptable standards of the society and this very much depends on education and culture of a particular country. But righteousness as related to God's requirements is a state of perfection required by God to enter Heaven which is an impossible demand from what man generally knows. Even many Christians do not quite understand what this really means. In the first place, if we do understand the Gospel aright, it abolishes forever all and every effort to obtain righteousness by fulfilling demands of Law – which are nothing but a moralistic delusion.

Doing all things required by law is simply an idiosyncratic belief or a terrible mistake which must be brought to the mind of every believer – a fixed false belief that man can fulfill God's righteous demands i.e. the righteousness demanded by God for anyone to enter Heaven by simply keeping Law's demands. This status is achieved only when God through the Gospel declares one righteous by His own forensic act through faith in Christ. This is the **positive advantage** revealed by the Word, the one and only means for removal of sins – **God's righteousness through faith in Christ.**

This is the astounding fact which no man on his own accord would have thought even possible to obtain the righteousness wholly apart from anything like Law (i.e. Mosaic Law or any other code such as human ethics).

- Men will always connect righteousness with Law of some kind and conceive it as consisting of "works of law."
- Yet all that Law is able to produce for sinners is conviction of sin, i.e. sin's realization – a conviction that all flesh, every mortal is damned and lost.

Here is the glory of God that there is another righteousness altogether apart from Law which is God's righteousness revealed in the Gospel i.e. the Law and the Prophets.

The source of God's Righteousness.
- Righteousness is brought about by faith in Jesus Christ which is for all those believing that Christ is the Savior, the instant one believes and as long as they continue believing.
- Faith is the heart's trust embracing Christ and by so embracing, it is the subjective means for making ours the status of righteousness, created by God's verdict, the bestowal of God's judicial declaration: "I declare thee righteous!" This declaration is ours where and when faith in Jesus Christ is ours.

No Law, just faith and yet God's own verdict is: Righteous! Righteous through faith – it is universal – as applying to anyone who puts his faith in Jesus Christ – upon all who are believing. The whole Old Testament as well as the New Testament both have ever attested to this righteousness as proceeding from God's verdict alone. It has ever been so from Adam onward – ever since Adam's fall there was never a righteousness, in, by and through law of any kind, it has always been "through, for, upon" faith apart from Law of any kind.
- Jesus and His apostles attested to the same truth, the mighty advantage which we have in the Word – (Romans 1:17) – our righteousness.
- Which is a manifestation of Christ on earth and testimony of the apostles – 3:21 which bring us this righteousness through faith.
- So faith is the medium through which we are declared righteous.

- On the other hand, faith is both the beneficiary (for all had sinned) and the subject upon the acknowledgment of God's Righteousness.

Three elements of faith:
a) As resulting from the Gospel (as witnessed by Jesus Christ and the Apostles.)
b) Having come to realization of our sinfulness as a result of law.
c) Pure declaration of a status of righteousness through faith.

In a world of sinners, anything like law only robs us of the favorable acknowledgment of God's verdict of righteousness. Then the big question remains, on what basis or what principle of fairness does God declare a sinful person righteous?
- Thank God – He meets this apparently hopeless situation.
- He declares righteous by means – "gratuitously" (free of charge) – by His own means declaring righteous – despite the universal sinfulness of man, we are not hopelessly lost under the verdict of guilty. God declares righteous in a wonderful way – wholly by means of Grace alone – that is Christ's death and faith.

3) The Gospel is Our Ransom (Salvation)

God is able to extend favor. In fact He does extend the greatest favor to all sinful men by Grace mediated through the ransom connected with Jesus Christ. This declaration of righteousness to a believer is the Gospel justification – which finds us miserable sinners all to whom it comes and clothes us in its garment, all the destitute sinners upon whom it comes. Here we see how far the promise of the Gospel extends: as far as sin extends, that is; all over the whole world.

- God's verdict is pronounced by way of a gift, it could not be pronounced in any other way, for the entire world of sinners, not one mite of merit existed – the gratuity is absolute (good, sufficient, pleasing and complete). In this way it fits every manner of sinfulness – the faith is central to personal justification, and no personal justification ever takes place except through faith. Grace is the inner motive that moved God to acquit. (Christ and the apostleship) – The ransom.

This appears and sounds like God being moved to declare a sinner righteous whose sin cries to him for just punishment – this is possible for only one reason; the one that perfectly satisfies God's justice and opens the way for His Grace through the ransoming, the one connected with Jesus Christ. The ransoming, the act that secures release by paying a ransom. Only the payment of a full ransom released the sinner in God's court.

- It is God as the agent, who gratuitously gave the gift i.e. makes him the "Bestower" of that grace through "ransoming." God declares righteous those with faith because of His ransom connected with His Son.

Ransom – God set forth Christ Jesus as cover or lid of the mercy seat to be effective through faith in connection with Jesus' blood – a reference to things relating to the Tabernacle and its worship. Christ's blood covered those mercy seats: it was the expiratory blood which covered the sins of the people from God's punishment. God Himself established the Jewish Tabernacle, the Ark and its mercy seat, so He was the one who also set forth their anti-type Christ, as a mercy seat; and both of these He connected with Blood.

Jesus the mercy seat!

It is Christ's very obedience unto death the very satisfaction, the very thing which is imputed to us for righteousness. By this act God punished all the sins committed since Adam's day to the present time and to the end of the world, in Christ. Christ is our mercy seat to whom our faith can cling.

The basis of God's righteousness consists in the justifying act of God which declares believers righteous and puts them unto that status. So it is not a mere attribute of God. God set forth Christ as the mercy seat. This righteousness was manifested all along as witnessed by the Old Testament Scripture: a type of mercy seat existed all along in the Ark of the Tabernacle.

God passed over their sins (salvation). They believed what the Word testified i.e. God pardoned all the sins of the Old Testament saints (Psalm 32:1–2). But what actually took away the sins of the Old Testament saints was Christ's Blood until that blood was actually shed, all remission of sins was "a passing over." The final ransoming of the sins was postponed until the actual antitype, mercy seat was set forth. No wonder all of them longed for Christ to come (Matt 13:17, John 8:56).

Christ's blood was the actual act of our High Priest entering into the Holy of Holies of Heaven with His own Blood (Hebrews 9:12,24). The actual demonstration of God's justifying righteousness by setting forth Christ as the mercy seat, i.e. in and through Him.

The great result:
So God's setting forth Christ as the mercy seat – is what is referred to as "He is righteous" declaring the believer in Jesus. So we have this revelation in (Romans 1:17) that God "declaring righteous" and that he is righteous in declaring a believer righteous. Faith and faith alone has God's righteousness.

God used a principle that completely eliminated all and any category of the works; any moralism or obedience to any law, be it the Mosaic code of Laws, God discarded any principle that might recognize them. Even works of faith – they are also to be shut out from justification, these works follow faith and justification, which is entirely complete before these good works ever appear or are even possible.

True, the works of faith justify (James 2:24) and not faith only "devoid of these works," which is dead in itself. The conclusion from all this – is our doctrine of the justification put into the form of a confession – and this Gospel is the only seal of Salvation for man.

We reckon, meaning "we believe, teach and confess." God has produced this conviction in us. There is overwhelming evidence for this in both Testaments. This is the one central doctrine of the entire Bible, with which also the Church stands or falls – centered in this Word. Justification by faith is our conviction and confession as well.

ROMANS CHAPTER 4:1-25
The Gospel is Sovereignty of God

Here is God's gracious gift to mankind; His sovereignty, His governance which;
1) Substitutes believers' faith for righteousness
2) Establishes the spiritual quality
3) Establishes the hope of our resurrection

1) The Gospel Power – Substitutes believers' faith for righteousness

All men should know one thing, it is not the transgression of law that is the result of sin, but ungodliness – (Romans 1:18.) Men would not have God rule them with His rule of Grace. Man does not recognize God as divine and with absolute power – the Creator. God has revealed Himself in countless ways to man: nature, providences and gifts of love etc. This beneficence would have led men to seek God and find Him revealed in the Gospel which would kindle faith in their hearts.
- Thus godless they became and this is the sin of ungodliness and the root and source of all unrighteous conduct with God's verdict of eternal death.

Paul introduces the wonderful quality of a new life which is faith in Christ; which alone God recognizes as righteous-

ness. Unfortunately few men know about this quality of a new heart.
- The faith or Christ in the heart restores God's character in men and this is the restoration of godliness in their hearts through the gift of the Holy Spirit.
- To this faith in Christ, God declares the person with such faith Righteous. This is justification through faith – it is the right to exist. Without faith you have no right to exist, no matter what the world says, you are condemned to eternal death.

Justification through faith is the righteousness which is witnessed (or evidenced) in the whole of the Old Testament Scriptures. In fact it is the one great theme of all the Scripture from Genesis to Revelation in the New Testament.

It is for this reason Paul considers the case of Abraham who dominates the Old Testament and to whom the New Covenant was promised.
- Abraham dominates the Old Testament and even God names Himself "the God of Abraham." It is He who stands out as the father of all believers because of this Righteousness or "justification through faith" alone. Faith in Christ alone acquits a sinner from sin and death. Man uses law for change of behavior but it doesn't work. It is in fact the falsehood of man.

Man everywhere relies on Law to produce the standard behavior according to the Law such as the Ten Commandments or the constitutions of each individual nation.
- This is an issue that disturbs many Christians, and makes many fall from God's Grace for not knowing what righteous standards God demands. So sinfulness is lack of faith in Christ – and this is the sin of the entire world.

- The Jews put Christ (the Gospel power) to death, because they did not believe Him to be the Savior, the Messiah, the Son of God and the Promised One. And this is their sin to this day – it is also the sin of the world. Lack of faith in Christ is the evidence of ungodliness or the sin of the world. It is the very disregard of the divine saving power.

Abraham believed God and this was reckoned to him as righteousness, and as such he is the supreme example of God's righteousness. He was justified by faith – (James 2:23) meaning faith produced the only quality of life which God wants and demands from everyone.

Justification is righteousness through faith. But how can faith be accounted as righteousness or everlasting life apart from works, and when did God so reckon or declare without any works done? Abraham's justification is recorded in Genesis Chapter 15 long before he proceeded to offer Isaac as a sacrifice – which is recorded in Genesis Chapter 22.
- This accounting is substitution, faith is the object for which God accounts for righteousness.
- But how and why does God reckon, in such a manner? Someone not working but faith alone and is declared righteous, (Romans 3:24)
- What then is there in faith or in a believer? No virtue or merit, nothing of this sort to the end of his life and then he is declared righteous? This is incredible!!

Something else, entirely different which God looks at. The contents of his faith, Christ, His ransom, His merit. The faith that holds Christ, God counts for righteousness and no other faith. The substitution takes place right here. Abraham's faith was so reckoned.

- God has no workers to whom He ever pays. Only men can hire, yes only men make that such reckoning (i.e. pay for work done). God does not make that kind of reckoning or pay.

God simply reckons faith for righteousness and there is no such reckoning among human beings. But how logical, reasonable and true can such reckoning take place? Giving His Son for our ransoming which has no human parallel, so also is His declaring the believer righteous and is without a human counterpart.
- This type of counting faith for righteousness constitutes the Gospel mystery which had to be revealed and can be received only as it is supernaturally revealed. Man not working but declared righteous – almost unbelievable!
- The object of faith is Jesus Christ which also includes the act of justification. This faith is not merely believing but the possession of Christ by faith for righteousness. Faith therefore is not an act by man, but God's Gospel power – the content of which is God's wrought faith – thus and thus only does God reckon it for righteousness.
- Thus and thus only is a believer declared righteous; meaning he has received the gift of eternal life – as a result of having Christ in his heart.

2) Establishes the spiritual quality

Sin dismissed:
Example of David's certainty – his faith was strong indeed: "Blessed!" the Hebrew exclamatory, but our version converting it into an assertion – blessedness;

The spiritual condition resulting from justification through faith – "sin removed" – new life, new spirit – and we should note the relation to the removal of ungodliness, thereby godliness enters.

1st: **Iniquity** dismissed – literally **lawlessness**, once as **rebels**, from birth revolted against God; i.e. godlessness – 1:21 – our original definition of sin.

- "We will not have this man reign over us" the Jews told Christ and the Lord answered it "bring them hither and slay them before me." (Luke 19:14, 27)
- This is the criminal refusal to come up to the divinely set mark i.e. God's Gospel of faith or the divine law. This is the godless heart, the rebellious action of abolishing such a mark, and setting up one that pleases the sinner better, not only by mouth but by deed.
- The road of godly right, of willing obedience to God's law (faith) is despised: we have turned everyone to his own way – (Isaiah 53:6) – each one with his own god in godlessness, each one makes his own laws, his worship etc.
- The three terms together (iniquity, lawlessness, rebellion) amount to the guilt of man, the same applies to the removal of this guilt and the three below constitute the heart of the Gospel, i.e. "**Dismissed**," so great is this blessed act to which David adds another, godliness has entered through faith.

- Were **covered** by the Blood of Jesus, our mercy seat; i.e. sins removed, justification by faith.
- And the Lord will in "**no wise reckon**" our sins, Righteousness, new life in man restored.

Secondly; The seal of righteousness (Baptism):
Apart from this blessedness of the sins removal: there is the seal of righteousness. Abraham was justified long before he was circumcised: His faith alone justified him.
- We are the true children of the father of believers because we too having been justified by the same means, him being the first.

For us of the Gentile origin, the Holy Spirit is the seal by the sign of Baptism with which we are sealed in attestation that we are saved, Ephesians 1:3, Abraham's seal of circumcision was such a seal of attestation (confirming the truth).

Righteousness is invisible, for God's verdict is pronounced in the secret chambers in heaven: hence we have the seal, circumcision in the Old Testament to which was added the Passover, but in the New Testament we have Baptism as the seal to which was added the Lord's Supper.

So we Christians stand in Abraham's faith, in the tracks of his faith, the counts (reckoning) of his faith recorded in Scripture – and as such Righteousness through faith, Christ is ours and so is the assurance of our salvation.

Thirdly: The fulfillment
(Death and Resurrection of Christ):
- The covenant which proceeded from God to Abraham meant that Abraham was to be the Father of all believers.
- He could be such a father only through faith.

- At first, when he was still in the foreskin – before he was circumcised, and thereafter, received circumcision as a seal.
- But this subjective means of faith has its objective means. Faith has its own objective basis.
- This basis could not be anything resembling law, it had to be and it was ever; **The Promise of Christ.**

This promise could and did produce and enable the faith first in Abraham and thus in all believers whom he was the spiritual father.

The great promise to Abraham and to His seed – namely that he is the heir of the heavenly world – through Christ. God did not attach it to Law; Law would have been the wrong vehicle.

- Law could never have made either Abraham or his seed righteous and they had to be made righteous in order to have this Promise and to have it fulfilled in them, faith in Christ.
- For if they had been left in an unrighteous state, they would have been no better than all the rest of mankind.
- Abraham and his seed had to be made righteous.

They were and are made so "**by means of faith's righteousness**." And as such they became the heirs, the future possessors by means of inheritance, after it has been cleansed and made a new earth. The world is Abraham's, his alone, and through him ours too – those who have believed.

But those of the Law, those only circumcised, the unbelieving Jews who reject the Gospel and seek righteousness by means of the Law – made empty have been their faith. Law rules out both this faith and the Promise on which it rests; the one which first kindled it.

What then is Law or what does it do?
There are many who think that they shall inherit the world by Law or works. (3:20)
- Instead of being declared righteous and thus made heirs, Law works only by the realization of sin. (3:20) Law cannot make us heirs.

Sadly there is no place anywhere on earth where there is no law, where there is no transgression and where there is no wrath that follows. It is the reverse, namely that there is no place here where Law is not present and does not reveal sin as what it is i.e. transgression of Law. In short:

Law is everywhere, thus sin is everywhere – this is the blow for all humanity to hang on the Law. Thus faith is never without righteousness as it is never without the Promise of Christ.

So the term "out of faith" as opposed to "through the law" – has two components;
1. Regarding the Gospel which is our gift of righteousness.
2. Regarding our personal faith, which is our justification through faith.

The fulfillment was Grace.

Grace was God's part through His own Son; a part that was glorious for Him and blessed for us beyond anything that language is able to express – Christ's work on the Cross.

No wonder God intended it so! In fact as we read elsewhere, God intended that no man shall ever doubt that pure grace is the norm of His entire saving work – 3:24 through His own Son.

Since everything is "out of faith in Christ" and thereby intended to be derived from Grace, the great result attained is spiritual life (our certainty) through the Holy Spirit or the

Word. So the divine promise is sure for all the seed, sure and certain for their conviction and not merely on God's part. All that the promise needs is faith, and even the tiniest faith avails fully.

3) Establishes the hope of our resurrection

This grand fatherhood of Abraham which included the Gentile believers together with the Jewish believers is the same truth that was uttered by God Himself to Abraham in Genesis 17:5, when God changed his name from Abram (father of height) to Abraham, father of multitudes, and also stated the reason – "for a father of many nations have I made thee." "I have established thee as the father of many nations" which goes back to Genesis 12:3, 15:5 and to the counsel (sovereignty or governance) of God, which lies back of this passage.
- In God's eyes, Abraham had long been a father of many nations although Isaac had not been born at this time; and both Abraham and Sarah had lost all procreative power.
- Strange, indeed, was this Promise (13,16) for to Abraham's ears it was pure promise.
- Seeming incredible, yet it asked for nothing but faith, for a promise can be received in no other way (Law is different) and it prompted faith, for it is the very nature of promise to produce faith.

And surprisingly Abraham believed and he did not waver because of unbelief (Vs. 20). He believed and that was the great

deed. He also believed God as One who makes alive the dead and calls the non-existing things as existing. It is such a God that Abraham believed in.
- Such a God he saw in the "I" who told him he had been made father of many Nations and therefore his Name was to be Abraham instead of Abram.
- This was Abraham's conviction as he had it when God spoke to him.

Abraham's conviction reached much farther – even the vivifying (give new life) of both their bodies – He believed in the resurrection, in the fact that God is able to bring the dead back to life – (Hebrews 11:19). Thus as father of many nations, it really involved also much more.
- Making alive his and Sarah's dead bodies so that through theirs and Isaac's line Christ could be born – faith in the sovereignty of God is the spiritual life.

The spirituality (certainty – hope resting on the Word)
- Christ through whom alone Abraham was the spiritual father, as now already existing – all required the faith of Abraham.
- And in God's eyes they (the many nations) were existing in God's sight. He had already called them, Abraham had already been constituted as their father. Abraham saw all that was involved in being such a God – he believed what God said.

The many nations of whom Abraham is the spiritual father are Abraham's spiritual children through God's calling, the call of Grace by the Gospel making them such children – this too Abraham saw – V18.

All was "beyond hope" as far as Abraham's and Sarah's bodies were concerned: but "on hope" rests everything on **God's Word** which is the Promise.
- The result was that by this act of believing, he became the father of many nations (in Christ) in accord with what had been declared in Genesis 17:5 (Father of many nations – the many stars so shall thy seed be) and already in Genesis 15:5.

Thus shall be thy seed. What God did in His counsel became a historical fact the instant Abraham believed the result there and then was attained.

Looking at the Promise of God and V17 of His great fatherhood of both Jews and Gentiles, he became strong with faith – i.e. "being fully persuaded that what He had promised He is able to perform," no matter what seeming impossibilities that promise may involve. (Like making alive the dead and like calling the non-existent as existent.)

To be fully persuaded – is to believe; literally to be full of faith – a reference to the special promise made to Abraham, but Abraham's persuasion covered more, namely that God is able to perform anything and everything that He has ever promised anyone at any time.

So it is this faith, this believing being what it was "it was reckoned unto him for righteousness." What is reckoned as righteousness is Christ, the substance of faith and heart of the Promise to Abraham.

The record of Abraham is the sacred writ – the Holy Spirit for our own sake so that we may read and know how we are justified exactly as he was, thus live a life worthy of the call.

By divine reckoning Abraham was justified. By the same divine reckoning all believers are justified and in no other way. Thus for our own sake too, it was written, since he is our spiritual father, and we his spiritual children too, whom, to our faith "shall be reckoned righteous." Our justification is a divine reckoning just as Abraham's was.

The promise given to Abraham's faith has now been fulfilled and the crown of this fulfillment being – God having raised Jesus our Lord from the dead. This resurrection of Christ was the fulfillment of the promise to Abraham, is the basis of our faith as it was and as it will be; the basis for all new covenant believers. He was raised from death, His sacrifice sufficed, God set His seal upon Him by raising Him up.

It is whom God delivered up on account of our "transgressions;" sins revealed and brought out as what sin really is. This atoning death is joined with the resurrection, was raised up on account of our being declared righteous, the act which produces the quality and justification for deliverance from our sins. Our transgressions and our being declared righteous speak of believers alone, because in them the purpose of God's counsel is fulfilled. To have such faith (repentance and Christ) is to receive the gift of the Holy Spirit. It is to be governed by God's sovereignty. – The hope of our resurrection.

ROMANS CHAPTER 5:1-21
God's Love is Fulfillment of the Law

The Gospel is God's Love (our fulfillment of the Law.) The Love of God and that of His Son brought the greatest rescue – "the Gospel of Christ." The vicarious death which brought about the removal of sin and death, reconciled the whole world but not without justification through faith. God's love consists of the following elements;
1) Our Deliverance – Christ's obedience.
2) Our Redemption – the vicarious death.
3) Our Hope – the gift of the Holy Spirit.

This chapter brings all scriptural terminology together for our understanding of the source of life;
Sin and death
Unrighteousness
Righteousness
Difference between Law and "the Law"
Justification
Reconciliation
Ungodliness
Grace
Vicarious death
Condemnation
Faith
Redemption
Eternal life
Spiritual life
The Gospel

God's Love
Salvation
Passion
Sacrifice
The Resurrection

1) Our Deliverance – Christ's Obedience

Man is in a state of confusion, he lacks the vital knowledge which enables every individual to move safely into the **true life**. True life is that which passes on to **eternity** after the **physical death**. The vitality of life we know is only a spark which flickers for a little while and it is gone for good with no **hope of resurrection**. True life starts with the **knowledge of sin**. It is this life which Paul unfolds in this Chapter, and with this **new life** Paul sweeps through the world age from Adam to the last day, from one border of eternity to the other, with Christ being in the centre. This is the real theology – the study of the one true God.

There are factors which cannot be denied such as **the universality of sin**, and its **cause of death**. The origin of sin is not merely empirical but actual. Its occurrence is well known and in most cases leaves no one to live beyond 100 years, at least, most of the time. **The origin of Sin** poisoned all living things and so doomed all in advance. The way in which sin and death entered the world left no possibility of escape for any man. God looked down and found all humanity in their **sinfulness**. The one sin that infected all men is the **ungod-**

liness; man is born **in flesh**, that is, with no **knowledge of God** the Creator – (Romans 1:18).

Man should have appreciated **the Creator** – God and all His providences, the whole work of creation etc. but suppressing this quantum of knowledge of all God's providences is the **ungodliness of man** revealing hearts without knowledge of the true God. Because of this ungodliness, God visits His **retribution** including **eternal death** to all men.

This ungodliness – is the sin of the world and already existed in Adam and was revealed when Adam was given the one commandment. It was exceedingly easy to obey only one particularly simple law, but because of the sin of ungodliness, Adam transgressed even this one particular law. The sin of ungodliness is born within us the instant we come into flesh. Thus the whole race in the loins of Adam was condemned to eternal death. What the law served in the case of Adam was to reveal the sin of ungodliness, and to this day Law can only reveal sin, but cannot change man for the better. We should also note that during the period between Adam and Moses, there was no law such as the Ten Commandments. This period ended with the coming of the Law of Moses, yet the sin was already in the world – a deadly power i.e. there was death even without any particular law.

The sin of ungodliness together with this one transgression of the one commandment, death came into the world. It went through all men who were not yet born.
- This death reigns like an absolute monarch, it needs no law and all that law can do is to reveal this power. And so we have death even at the very birth of a child!
- Thus Able was killed by his brother (evidence of sin) and so every one of the ancients ends in death.

God's **condemnatory verdict** to all our ungodliness is **eternal death**. Death reigns through the sin just the same, whether some law has been transgressed or not. There would have been no man living had it not been for the act of the one Man who is prefigured by Adam. Adam's fatal act typifies Christ's act of deliverance in a certain vital way, the latter had to undo the former.

- Jesus is prefigured by so many types and even when all are taken together, they can only indicate a bit of His greatness.
- Adam destroyed himself and all others, Christ wrought His gracious gift only for others, He did not need it for Himself, it was His gift to us all.
- No gain was there for Him to be tested, such as the one law which Adam had failed to pass but Christ won for Adam and for all of us the full reign of **life everlasting**.
- "**The status of righteousness through reconciliation.**"

So grave was the inexcusable fall of Adam (ungodliness) that it killed all men so that hope of deliverance, at the time seemed gone forever. So the grace of God and the gift in connection with grace of the one Man Jesus Christ, both are purely unmerited favor, both brought about the great rescue.

One man who is God's Son is here united with God in the bestowal of exceeding grace – the power that reaches out to save the guilty ones who deserve only death. Adam's fall was the sin of ungodliness – kills all, an adverse verdict and our condemnation. But now the **graciousness of God** and the **gift in connection with grace of Jesus Christ**: the wonder of wonders – the exact opposite of Adam's sin – **the verdict of justification through faith.**

- A blessed acquittal right out of many falls, not only Adam's fall but all the rest including our own fall as a result of our

ungodliness. This is what the divine Judge who is God does to those who have believed in Christ's work of Salvation.
- With Adam's sin (ungodliness,) one verdict of condemnation, and so the verdict declaring righteous establishes righteousness through faith – as a result of God's Grace and that of Jesus Christ.
- The fact that God announces a verdict of condemnation on Adam's sin is as natural and right as it can be.
- We accept this verdict without further thought as a matter of course. But it sounds impossible and incredible, that God should pronounce a verdict that is the direct opposite, a verdict of acquittal and righteousness when He has before Him all the falls of all men through faith in Christ.
- Impossible and yet a fact; incredible and yet true – the reason and basis: is **personal forgiveness** for sins for every individual and all men in the world. All men were reconciled to God, call this **universal or world justification**, but never in the sense of absolving every individual sinner of his sin before faith and without faith – i.e. only to those who are receiving the abundance of grace, God promises the declaration of righteousness the instant faith is kindled. In the fall, death reigned as an absolute monarch through Adam – a verdict of condemnation reigned over all men.
- Now the status of righteousness produced by the verdict of righteousness to only those who have received the abundance of grace – faith in Jesus Christ, on all who have believed – the restoration of the godliness of God and Christ in the heart.
- This receiving is only the means to the real and ultimate end: In life shall we reign through the One Jesus Christ. Eternal Life is the goal of **Justification by faith**. The justified are not only freed from that death but are transferred

unto Life Eternal, they are to attain the goal which Adam was to attain originally.
- Adam's disobedience making many sinners; Christ's obedience making many righteous through faith.
- Sin and death have one source – Adam.
- Righteousness and life also have one source – the second Adam – Christ's obedience. So through faith in Christ, we receive eternal life.

2) Our Redemption – The vicarious death and the Reconciliation

- The manifestation of God's love is by grace alone. There has never been a righteous person before or after Jesus' act of death. There has been only one category of sinners "the ungodly ones" – in which we are all born as enemies of God.
- We are not merely sinners who missed the mark set by law, and not merely unrighteous ones who fail to meet the norm of right embodied in law, but ungodly ones.
- Those who are hostile to God. This term ungodly goes to the root of sin. It is as such men who fill up the whole world whom Christ died for.
- The one class of all living and all who have ever lived are all classified as being ungodly, Christ died for all such as these ungodly ones and is the one class of human race.

There was not a bit of difference among men, all locked up in the one sin of ungodliness, generation after generation.

It is this vicarious death of Christ which effectively removes the ungodliness for those who later become justified through faith. It is a death for all the ungodly who also include all believers who were once in their ungodliness, from Adam onwards, to the present day and the future – the very history of man from eternity to eternity.

Ungodliness is the characteristic of all of them before they believe. The fact that Christ's death occurred at a specific time in history makes no difference as far as its relation to ungodliness of even believers is concerned.

- It is an established fact that Christ's death was vicarious. He died as the substitute instead of us all who are full of ungodliness.
- Christ could and did die for all the ungodly mass of the world. He laid down His life and could and did ransom all of them. Rarely will a human being die for another, much more difficult for a criminal, a sinner. Here now is the contrast; God commends His own love to all the ungodly in that, while we were still in our ungodliness, Christ died for us all; he died in our place. In other words there would not have been a living soul on earth today.
- So far God's love does exceed the utmost limit of human love. So far the self-sacrifice of Christ exceeds the highest of human readiness for self-sacrifice.

This is the love of God that has been poured out in our hearts through the Holy Spirit.

Commending – place in the right (favorable) light for full acceptance, this commendation is by the **Spirit, by means of the Gospel with its substance which is Christ.**

As God's love – it constitutes the sending of His Son so that He might come into the hour of His Passion (John 12 etc.) and His death was voluntary, of His own will, the acme of self-sacrificing love: the Lamb of God dying voluntarily for the ungodly ones. This love of God makes Christ the Great Mediator of **Salvation** of all the **justified**. And justification is the supreme result, which is salvation. Christ died to save the **ungodly** from the wrath which their **ungodliness** merits. By our enmity, our sins, our ungodliness, we had gotten ourselves into a desperate status that deserved nothing from God but wrath, penalty and damnation.
- That unless God did something to change this status, it could compel Him to treat us thus i.e. condemned as he did with Sodom and Gomorrah.

Thus by means of Christ's death God changed this into an utterly different status, one that despite our enmity etc. to go on commending to us His love, this very love changed that status. This love compelled Christ to die for us hostile enemies of God – it took the sacrificial death of His Son to do it.

God reconciled us and the whole world. The instant Christ died, the whole world of sinners was changed completely. It was now a world whose sins had been atoned for and no longer one of the un-atoned sins. Though it is over 2000 years ago, His death is ever effective – (Revelation 3:8). His atonement and reckoning are valid for the universe of men. This objective act affected through Christ for the whole world, is to be followed by the subjective act in each individual – through the ministry of reconciliation.
- "The Word of the reconciliation" calling to us: "Be ye reconciled to God." (2Corinthians 5:18–21) This is a second and different act, it too is wrought by the Word of God but

now makes the individual other by changing his enmity unto faith – and thus Paul states;

"We have received the reconciliation" i.e. we have received it by faith. So from the greater one, the death of God's Son and to the less reconciliation of us His enemies through that faith. The final saving us all, the reconciled ones, **in connection with Christ's life** – His Resurrection, shall be saved.

God is the agent in all the three actions, reconciled by God through Christ's death, declared righteous by God, saved by God through faith. God is the agent throughout – salvation is the great result of justification. Our salvation is the overwhelming certainty.

And on this immense ground of our faith rests our "hope of glory" in which we boast with hearts elate make us so happy, joyful and proud.

The blood of animals, their repetition alone could not take away the sins, it could only symbolize and typify the blood of the Son. The blood of the Son shed once brought about eternal atonement, effected in the Holy of Holies in heaven. The Son's death and blood destroyed death so that He arose to glory in life, so that even as He arose to glory in life, that even as He lives, we shall live also.

- So we shall be saved, the last consummation of our hope, the final completion of our hope – Salvation (the Resurrection).

So the reconciliation was effective for the whole world of sinners and changed our status from the unredeemed to the redeemed. Our status as redeemed does not save anyone until it is bestowed (reconciliation) and received individually through faith – unbelief rejects the reconciliation and thus the individual perishes. This is tragedy indeed! The reconciliation consists of the two saving acts; i.e. **the removal of Sin** and **the removal of** eternal Death – by the vicarious death, both of which are received only through faith in Christ. But we who by faith clasped this reconciliation to our hearts were justified because of it, sing praises to God, and all our exultation is made possible "through our Lord Jesus Christ" through whom God reconciled us to Him.

3) Our Hope – the gift of the Holy Spirit

We always talk of the new life – most of the time it is not understood as to what is exactly meant, but this cannot be the case where the experience is true and real.
- Life in a new born baby is the cry, noise and all manner of movement experienced, with its source, the mother being at hand to enhance its development. New Life in Christ – is the spiritual life – Paul describes it in a metaphysical (graphical) manner.

He who is led through the golden portal of faith, God's declaration of righteousness descending upon him as he enters, thereby passes into the divine city of life and there we find the riches of that blessed life.
- This true experience is all ours by justification through faith or having received the reconciliation. Justification – the feeling of having been declared righteous, all our sins removed, for what reason? Simple answer! Faith in Jesus

Christ our Lord, who is the substance of our faith – this is the only true quality of God's own righteousness that avails spiritual life or eternal life in our hearts.

Not only having been declared righteous through faith in Christ Jesus our Lord as a result of His sacrificial death and blood, this is only half the story, but also His resurrection is the second half of the story – which is now the great hope of all believers, the resurrection because He who is the substance of their faith has too resurrected.

So Christ is the base of our grand hope of the glory of God. The fullness of this glory will be revealed at the consummation – at the end of the world.

So the main activities of this spiritual life are;
1) Righteousness.
2) The Great Hope.

1) Righteousness

Peace namely; to have and enjoy the feeling of peace (Here too is the substance of the believer's heart with which St. Paul greets the Church in Rome: "**Peace to you.**" And here among us, "Let us have peace" having been pronounced righteous by God, which he has established for us objectively (not a result of our works but His).

- God has established the condition of peace by removing all our sin and our guilt; all of His wrath is turned from us, all His grace rests upon us.
- God is at peace with all the righteous ones, the justified. This peace all believers should experience.
- Peace is the dismissal of any fears that He holds anything against us because of what Christ has already mediated for us.

What Christ has mediated, the entrance has been made "by faith" into this grace in which we stand. Faith is the glorious portal that is waiting open to be the entrance through which by faith we pass into this grace. Now see, He who now mediates "peace" for us "also" mediates this entrance into this grace.

2) Our Hope

Here is our glory, here is our praise, our greatness, our nobility for what we are waiting for: the consummation at the end of the world which will be our final, glorious great Hope. This hope like the peace, both rest on the Mediator Christ, on the eternal Word of Promise. Here really is our glory – the realization of the Truth in God's Word.

"Our glory" (in the sense of God's acknowledgement of us) of which our sinning makes us fall short, faith given through Christ, namely, the blessed acknowledgment of God that we are righteous – no hope is needed for that, we have been justified.

- Next is the glory for which we hope for God's blessed attributes when He completes His saving work in us by raising us from the dead, uniting our souls and our bodies, and then ushering both into the kingdom prepared for us. So the gap between now and the end, God aids us in the following ways:

a) **Affliction** – So for the intervening period – all affliction – pressure that comes to Christ's believers through the hatred of the world are used by God as the means to draw us near to Him.
    - Afflictions step by step carry us upward to the great hope that does not put us to shame.
    - The remaining under the load without complaining or faltering and goes right on no matter what the load may become.

b) **Tried condition of faith** – Then the load produces perseverance, a tried condition of not wanting and so we reach this tried condition of our faith, a glorious condition indeed which cannot be reached in any other way in this world of sin.

c) **And the third step: this tried condition of hope, the subjective personal assurance concerning the future and the fulfillment of God's Promises,** the great courage that remains firm in all affliction – we reach the New Testament Hope – which is the prospect of a condition that satisfies all needs, fills all wants, frees us from all of life's hindrances, viz (namely) consequences of sin, – a satisfying superseding the unsatisfying present, on the basis of the believed promises and facts of salvation.

In fact, the whole Old Covenant was built on hope, redemption now realized and this much hope fulfilled. The consummation still remains to make the New Covenant glorious with **hope**. And this hope does not put to shame! Because there is something that guarantees the fulfillment of our hope, guarantees it beyond question – it is the love of God, poured out in our hearts through the Holy Spirit. He Himself being no longer outside of us but having been given to us and now dwelling in our hearts. The love of God fulfilment our hearts, God's gift to us guarantees the fulfillment of our hope of glory of God. The instant when God declares us righteous – we realize the power by means of the Word. And the essential effect of this righteousness which is eternal life and our being saved – therefore we shall be saved.

ROMANS CHAPTER 6:1-23
The Gospel is our Deliverance

God created the world with everything in it, including man himself i.e. Adam, with the stewardship of this world, placed firmly into the hand of man. Man rebelled, starting with Adam. Man refused to come to the full knowledge of the Creator God, he did not know God as the Creator. And this was the greatest sin of man from Adam onwards. Men's hearts were filled with ungodliness and that led to God's condemnation of the world to eternal death. To restore His eternal purpose – **God's love was revealed** in the gift of grace which brought about **the redemption, the restoration of God's plans for men** which consist of the following.
1) Our Liberation – Baptism.
2) Faith Obedience – Our Enslavement to Righteousness
3) Sanctification – the Spiritual body (unity)

1) Our Liberation – Baptism

There are certain things which all Christians must know as facts and believe them as they are. True facts acquired as knowledge transform men for their betterment, these simple facts unfortunately are missing in the minds of many believers, thus making it impossible to advance much in their spiritual lives. The basic fact we must all know is the **blessed**

power of grace, what it is, and what it has done for the human race. God's love and that of His Son produce the power of Grace. **This power is the sacrificial death of God's Son which ended the power of sin and death**, and to have this knowledge is to know the Creator.

Adam did not know his Creator, he lacked this basic knowledge and this was the sin: the ungodliness in the whole world. This ungodliness was revealed when Adam transgressed the one simple commandment he was given and from that moment death came into the world. Death was God's own condemnation of the world because of the sin of ungodliness. It is the power of grace, which is the most blessed and which produced the two major effects concerning the restoration of man.

a) Christ's death and Resurrection produced an end to the power of Sin and death.
b) It also produced the newness of life – one which only believers can experience, and fill their hearts with explicit joy and the two together form our liberation, the latter being a result of the former.

a) Christ's death – the removal of sin or ungodliness.
The sin, the ungodliness was the sphere in which all men moved, nothing in man could put this power of ungodliness to death, then came grace by the sacrificial death of the Son – and this sacrificial death is the power of grace – to repossess our souls through faith in Christ thus restoring the godliness. In other words, men who knew no God in their ungodliness, now they came to know God who entered their hearts through Baptism (the restoration of godliness through faith in Christ Jesus). We were baptized, we let ourselves be baptized, in connection with Christ, with His death and all His saving work – and what all this means, the instant faith is kindled by the power of Grace.

- Christ's mediation in connection with His sacrificial death, this sacrament, kindles the faith of the ungodly ones and instantly – there and then – God declares the sinner righteous (or justified,) to everyone whose faith in Christ has been kindled. Finally God entered their hearts and ungodliness was removed and thus sin and death ceased to exert their power (salvation.) Faith in Christ seals our connection with His sacrificial death; and our baptism is the full guarantee. Although it is only a sign of water but in the heavenly courts – it is a declaration of righteousness to every individual whose faith in Christ as the Savior is kindled. Thus faith in Christ is the only righteousness there is in the entire world in the sight of God.

In our baptism (faith) we died with Christ as regards the sin of the world and were entombed together with Him. This is a symbolic language representing a mystery or hidden meaning, – it was a dying together, the interval of time vanishes – **Christ's death was sacrificial (removal of sin) and vicarious in place of our own eternal death.** Our death with Christ is our escape from sin and eternal death and its dominion, the connection – faith or Baptism.

The function of this Sacrament of Baptism **is not to picture** or symbolize anything but to act as most effective divine spiritual means for the atoning death;
- **One that effects in us a death to the sin and a new life**, regeneration (John 3:5 and Titus 3:5) or new birth, thus the newness of life.

b) Spiritual Resurrection – Christ's resurrection – The New Life (End of the old man by God's Law.)

The immediate result of our death to sin is spiritual resurrection: similar to Christ's actual physical resurrection, and thus we come to walk in new life.

"Newness" – the opposite of our old fleshy life.

Our old man (our ungodliness) was crucified with Christ's crucifixion in baptism, He did not die willingly but was slain as one cursed of God, the agent was **the Law of God** as the means. The old man is our entire being as it existed before regeneration. Once for all it was put out of commission and so no longer functions as "the body of sin," in a helpless slavery under the sin power – but set free. Its members became servants of righteousness under our actual liberation – Verse 9.

With the sin dethroned, the new man has taken the place of the old man in us and now it is our task to prevent the sin from again usurping that throne. These are the great facts of our salvation. **These basic facts with all their blessedness are thus made personally ours by the death we die in baptism and our new life in Christ's resurrection – is our liberation.**

This knowledge of the liberating power and accepting it as true is;

- Our justification by faith, our acquittal from sin by the blessed power of grace and the beginning of a new life in Christ Jesus.

"In Christ Jesus" – the elements in which Christians move in connection with Christ Jesus must always go with our being dead to sin, as well as our living to God in our spiritual resurrection and these are the basic facts in which all believers of all the time must live: being dead to sin as well as our living to God is our obedience or enslavement to righteousness to which we now turn, as freed from the Law.

2) Faith Obedience – Our Enslavement to righteousness

The whole Christian life is obedience once for all, "from the heart." When one obeys he must have some teaching or some word to obey – that is the teaching of God which all Christians must come to obey known as the Christian teaching. This teaching includes both Old and New Testaments with its fulfilment that had come in Christ Jesus – the substance or the doctrine. We Christians were delivered and handed over to a new teaching whose content is a master whom we freely obeyed; we were made slaves to righteousness, obeying as slaves, as opposed to the old master – Satan who enslaved us by misuse of the Law.

The Teaching
It was no less than having our old man crucified with Christ's crucifixion by Pilate which crucifixion Jesus Himself wanted; i.e. to be crucified, dead and buried. We died with Him and were entombed with him for **our old sinful self was a terrible thing** and its very destruction we are ever thankful for – we ourselves wanted it and in this way we became slaves to righteousness. How did this happen? Through faith in Jesus Christ and the New Life. This is the obedience as slaves, obeying the voice of our Master God who speaks in this teaching. We obeyed from the heart as most willing slaves – the slavery which sets free by its enslavement. In this whole teaching we cease to be slaves to the sin and become obedient to Christian teaching. This is the obedience which includes **faith and thus new life, meaning regeneration.** This is the obedience of faith as opposed to the Law.

This form of teaching i.e. the Gospel in its entirety is very different from all other teachings such as adhering to law. It is new enslavement – enslavement to Righteousness as opposed to Law, this is our regeneration.

God delivered us over to the Gospel and thus enslaved us to righteousness, righteousness of a godly life – the glorious liberty we obtained when were made slaves to righteousness. "Emancipated from the sin" – that is liberty indeed. The sin power had stolen us from God by misusing of Law. We can now fulfil the purpose of our being free to obey our creator and Savior in newness of life. Our true place is with God, His will is our will. Even as a slave has no will of his own but his master's and his will for us is the faith's obedience.

- All these abilities are a result of the power of grace in Christ Jesus and thus the blessedness of our will which is one with God's will.
- Enslaved to righteousness is the obedience of faith – a power that is the opposite of the sin power and now we keep doing righteous works. Having been liberated from sin and now under His grace, we could not dream of letting ourselves slip back into sin!

Obedience of Faith sets us free from the Law!
Everyone is a slave to whom he keeps presenting himself for obedience. He is a slave to the master by choice and volition for obedience. This is definitely the case with Christians who by Baptism died to sin and were set free to live to God. Surely the very thought of obeying sin is wrong.

Obedience implies voluntary choice and conscious stooping to some sin, no Christian would think of voluntarily sinning and thus courting death – the tyrant death – impossible!!

Obedience is the opposite of sin. Slaves of God means obedient slaves of God. In life **our conduct can only be of sin or obedience i.e. slaves of obedience** who are only bent on nothing but obeying, who would not for a moment let go of obedience to which they wholly belong and have freely consciously made the choice, very different from sin enslavement which the Law reveals. Our obedience acts are pronounced righteous in God's courts (Matthew 24:34-40), heaven becomes ours through grace that is Christ's merits and faith which we reach by walking in the path of righteousness. So the Christian church from the very beginning is a course involved in the very nature of change that took place in obedience of faith. We were slaves to the sin, that hold of sin on us, the darkness then we became slaves to God or obedience of faith, spread out and thus by hearing became obedient from the heart to a form of teaching unto which we were delivered (i.e. rescued) – the faith or enslavement to righteousness. There and then we having been liberated from the sin, we were enslaved to righteousness – it is the Gospel teaching in which by God's grace "the Spirit" through the Word continues our obedience through faith and our enslavement to righteousness.

3) Sanctification – The Spiritual body (unity)

Our emancipation is a new enslavement. Before this emancipation we ever enjoyed a sad liberty – when we were slaves to sin. The sin power had usurped authority over us, stolen us from God and thus made us slaves.

- We never rightly belonged to this sin.
- We were not created for the sin power with its reign in death.
- We can now fulfill the purpose of our being – we now enjoy a glorious liberty which we obtained when we were enslaved to righteousness.
- We are free to obey our creator and our savior in newness of life. It would be contradictory to call this enslavement.

We never belonged to sin, **in addition we must serve God who is our Creator and Savior.** Our true place is with God, His will is our will, but all this belonging implies grace in Jesus Christ which in fact reveals the blessedness which is nothing but divine favor of our will which is one with God's will. God's blessedness (divine favor) has so bonded us to itself that we have become its most willing and happy slaves, slaves to righteousness "every work of ours being approved of God, joy and delight for us."

Now our liberty (our freedom, our will) is not a liberty to drop back into sin, but liberty that of our volition (ability of our own will) holds us to God and to righteousness, to such an extent as though He had completely made us His slaves. Sinners (slaves full of ungodliness) are ready to present their bodily members to the sin power as being so many slaves to do the sins bidding. Sin power; its effects can be referred to as the uncleanness or the lawlessness which are two aspects of sin.

All sin is abominable, it wrecks and stinks and does filth, and at the same time; it is a rebellion, anarchy, a challenge to law, that is what men do i.e. give one's own bodily members as slaves to such sin power by the use of Law. Too often we hide this horribleness from ourselves and shudder at it when it reveals itself stuck and naked in some fearful crime.

Lawlessness, this power itself grows the more when men lend their members as slaves, to do its will for uncleanness. Lawlessness exists as a vicious power.

Now all acts of giving our members "as slaves to righteousness" – obedience of faith, the opposite to the sin power. Keep doing, for the interest and augmentation of this blessed power; that is for the interest of God's work of setting us apart for himself also in conduct. The work of sanctifying us as regards our members is usually sanctification in a narrow sense. No man ever escapes the claims of righteousness; the freedom felt while under sin is only subjective freedom, the sinner merely disregards the righteousness. He feels elated not to be compelled to this or that but to be free to throw himself in vile arms of sin just as he pleases. You may want to call that freedom.

But what are the fruits at the end of such servitude? No fruits whatsoever! For the end of sin enslavement is eternal death. Now see, having been liberated from the sin and having been enslaved to God, we are having the fruit for sanctification (i.e. good works). It is entirely God who produced the fruit in us, which consists of virtues and graces that are implanted by Him (Galatians 5:22–24) and these foster His work of sanctifying us more and more. And finally the gracious gift of God is **life everlasting** in connection with Christ Jesus our Lord. Our work – service to God is the result of freely serving fellow believers, a relation among fellow believers – a service freely rendered and as we shall see later, which results in the full functioning of a spiritual body.

ROMANS CHAPTER 7:1-25
The Gospel is Our Redemption – (or God's Law)

God's law is written for both genuine Christians and for moralists. It is the inner biography of a genuine Christian who really knows what contrition is, from the fact of having experienced it and continuing to experience it. The truth is far from them, the source of trouble is the failure of the inward application of the Law and of the Gospel to the conscience and the heart until the normal experience of the power of both is achieved as it was in the case of Paul, the Christians in Rome and of course all others who have not merely heard about contrition and justification by faith but have the genuine experience of both. Without God's law there can be no salvation for man as he remains dead in flesh, without the knowledge of sin. Our deliverance from sin and death can only be effected by "the Law," God's own law which alone can bring about our:
1) Knowledge of Sin (Our Conversion)
2) Deliverance from the law (The Death of Christ)
3) The glorious hope (The New Spiritual Life)

To these effects of God's good law we turn our attention!

1) Knowledge of Sin – Our Conversion

Sin entered the world and its existence started right from the beginning with Adam; and this sin extended its power from then until this day. It is this sin power that was revealed by Adam through the one commandment that he transgressed. This transgression revealed Adam's sinful nature and brought about his death. It is this same Sin power which is behind all our lust. To this day man thinks that these lusts are perfectly natural and legitimate desires. Not at all! These are the result of sin – which lays dormant, in fact dead until a Law comes into effect.

One specific law – "*thou shalt not covet*" – not only lust but also passions are stirred up by means of this one Law, wich now is felt and becomes visible, as if irritated, thereby, and becomes active. Setup a law over unregenerate men and all kinds of passions are stirred up and become more active. Law seems to stir the fire so as to make flames flare in our hearts. These passions of sin, (these forces inside us) can only be awakened by any Law. It is folly to think that the Law kills these passions, it does the very opposite i.e. it acts as the medium for the revelation of these lusts which are driven by the sin power – which now become more active and work in our bodies as passions.

- It is these passions which are revealed by Law which bear the terrible fruit for eternal death.
- The Gospel of Christ is God's law which reveals this sin power – anything that reveals sin is law. This code of law written by God has greatly been misused – i.e. the specific laws such as the Ten Commandments have been taken as if intended for production of good works. It is a big

mistake. Its purpose is to reveal the sinful nature of man and then impress it upon our hearts.
- God's Law is written with mere ink, mere stone tablets, and mere laws outwardly imposed on man to reveal only the numeracy of our sin, our fall, our guilt; and can only make us obey it outwardly, not a new heart or spirit. Man cannot be changed by any outward means such as God's law which can only make his sins and guilt more visibly imposed on him i.e. can only increase his sin and guilt and can only make him obey outwardly at best, and only because of the dread of the penalty imposed. To obey the Law outwardly only increases the bondage – a hopeless bondage indeed and its end is death. So there is no such a thing as upholding the Ten Commandments. It is a big lie.
- The fears of the world, the thinking that without law it means lawlessness, license to break God's law and run wild in sin and crime is due to misunderstanding of what both Law and Gospel work is. The police power of government law can only restrain but cannot eradicate and there is no conflict between Law and the Gospel.
- The Law therefore is God's means of making a sinner conscious of his sin. Paul's own experience is very helpful in realizing exactly how he came to the realization of the sin power as the cause of death. Think of a specific sin such as "coveting" – who on earth does not have a desire for this or that thing? A new dress, a new car etc.?
- But this one sin of coveting cannot be understood as sin except through God's specific command against coveting. From the sin power – to one specific sin – coveting.

"Thou shalt not covet" the commandment which reveals the sin power of lust. The sin power – ungodliness is revealed as cov-

eting by God's law. Coveting is the source of some of the greatest crimes in the entire world – Ahab's coveting of Naboth's vineyard and all that followed afterwards. Everything that reproves sin is and belongs to law and leads to the knowledge of sin; the Ten Commandments are only an epitome of the Law and are known as God's good law.

- The Passion and the death of Christ are law in so far as they exhibit that sin inflicted suffering and death on Christ. So this is the whole mission of Christ in this sinful world.
- With this very prohibition not to covet, Paul became conscious of this very prohibition, the sin took hold of it and stirred Paul into all kinds of new violations – the poker in the hands of sin – the slumbering fire now shot out all its flames – like prodding a sleeping lion to rend. Any law stirs up sin (passions) and makes law show its power in producing "sin" motions and acts that have the quality of sin. Without law sin is dormant – it is dead.

Paul states, "There I was alive without Law" – meaning, all was quiet before the storm (Law) – when sin was quiescent in him, dead as he says. There was sin already in Paul's flesh – sin was quietly dormant, hidden in Paul's inner being – soul. In other words, quite secure amid all his sin and sinfulness. He lived in the sense that the death blow had not yet killed him. He sat secure in his house of ignorance like a man living on a volcano and thinking all is well.

- Today worldly ideas of morality protect many. Conscience is hushed, and even when the Law's thunders reach them, they succeed in stopping their ears and in feeling secure again.

Paul's security came to an end – with God's own prohibition. The "commandment" – "why are you persecuting me?" The result – the whole power of sin, got alive and "I died," Paul states. "For not only sin ceased to be dead but the sin power came alive," and so Paul died, his former living was brought to an end. The sin struck him dead with blow upon blow, again and again, and after every rally to get back into old security failed. *Then this death under law gave birth to another death, in that Paul died to both the sin and to the Law,* and then only reached the status of conversion. Paul's death to sin (or knowledge of his sins) is due to the death of Christ for the sin of the world. Paul is now connected to Christ through faith in Christ's saving work on the Cross.

It is not the commandment that killed Paul but the sin. And with Paul's conversion, he died to the sin. The true technical definition of conversion is; – our death to the sin. The death to the sin was brought about by Christ's own death for the sins of the world, now we live under grace, entombed with Christ.

2) Deliverance from the Law (The Death of Christ)

Deliverance from the Law is one of the fundamental effects of God's righteousness through faith in Christ Jesus. The things regarding law – should be a matter of general knowledge to all of us. Where law is binding only for life and not beyond death; this is the truth, that law never extends its jurisdiction beyond death. Everywhere on earth there is law, both among the educated and uneducated generally. Any person who knows anything at all about Law understands that all law and every law relinquishes its control at the time of death because the power of sin cannot animate the body and soul anymore. As believers it is a very important matter to understand our deliverance from law – so as to avoid legalistic minds which still persist in the minds of some brethren. There are many countless examples, and the best which highlights the new spiritual quality of a believer, the one which illustrates our death to the Law; this is our death to sin power which renders our release from law, whose purpose is only to reveal sin. The death of Christ is our release from sin and Law as well illustrated by the death of a woman's husband and this is our new spiritual life – the regeneration.

A husband's death abolishes their marriage and puts out the effect of her wifehood so that it is no more operative, now she is no longer under the Law of her marriage bands, she stands discharged from law and no more bound by it. Formerly she was under that law, now she is not under it anymore but is wholly set free from the Law of her former marriage.

The Truth
Here is the truth which Paul illustrates: a person may be entirely set free from a law without an overthrow of that law, revoking of that law, without anarchism or rebellion against that law. Yes indeed a person may be set free without an effort or an act of his own, he may be altogether passive, his release being accomplished by the death of another person who stood in a certain relation to the one set free. Of this nature is our freedom from the Law. It is not in the least wrong or questionable. The fears of legalists are at least wrong or questionable. These fears are unwarranted – they just need to look at this woman.

This truth is so exact because it refers to a death, one that ends one relation to open up another and to do that in the most legitimate way, and as such was the death of our Lord

Christ. So we Christians are no longer under law, we are now in the most blessed new relation: under grace – the woman's freedom from the law is the most perfect illustration.

This illustration is only a likeness. It is not a deduction expressed here. The death of Christ freed us from the law so that we belong to another, namely, to the Risen Christ our Savior.

- In both cases the death has to be that of a person who is so connected with another as to affect the liberation by this means alone.
- In the case of the woman her marriage to the husband.
- In our case, justification by faith makes the connections with Christ's liberating death from the law. Thus we are set free from the law by Christ's death just as her husband's death. More than this, **ungodliness** will have been replaced by godliness in our hearts. Our connection goes even further – we were rendered dead to the law, passive, we were set free; but only those who have the connection i.e. justification by faith alone have this spiritual benefit. We now belong to another, to the Risen Christ – just like the woman may now belong to another husband.

Christ's resurrection attests the all-sufficiency of His death and atonement, and only to this Risen Christ we belong in the fullest actuality born "for God" and for Christ. Under law we could only bear fruit for death, for law only increases the fall. Law does not produce any good works. Law is fatal for good works. For the Law never produced a single good work. Law always produces wrath – (Romans 4:15), it increases the fall (Romans 5:20), it works realization of sin (Romans 3:20) and never any good work.

- This analysis is to expose the fallacy of relying on law as the producer of good works. Here is the true meaning of

regeneration – death to the law so that we can bear fruits – which is our Sanctification. Fruits being our death to sin and our deliverance from the Law which is our belonging to Christ. These alone affect the purpose that we truly and actually bear fruit to God and the fruit is eternal life.
- Everything that is law, including the Mosaic Law, produces only fruit for death. This is when we are still in flesh, unconverted, not justified, not delivered from the sin – in our natural state of sin, the opposite of the spirit – in this state the passion of the sins, those (stirred up) by means of Law, continued to be active in our members to bear fruits for (unto) death.
- That is all that can be produced through the medium of law. With our deliverance from the Law, we can now bear fruit for righteousness – this is our new spiritual life for all who have believed in Christ Jesus our Lord.

3) The Glorious Hope – The New Spiritual Life

After conversion and regeneration, it is no longer a life that responds to the power of sin and death only, but a spiritual life where the power of sin has been driven out of the heart – the centre of our being, and now it remains only in the bodily members. We Christians have come to know the holiness of the Law not because it comes from God but more so for its wonderful purpose of revealing **the power of sin and death; and the grace of Our Lord.**

- The spiritual quality of the Law reveals our fleshiness – slavery to the sin and death, which is the complete make up of man before conversion, then also our living not under law but under grace.
- This fleshy nature, which is also known as the old nature still remains in the converted even after conversion.
- So believers are not fully rid of this flesh (old man) and this is the cause of the entire **conflict with the spiritual law** of God among the converted.

Saved from the sin and death by God's own righteousness (Christ) through faith, this emancipation still left flesh in Paul. And the flesh that was still left was no better flesh than it had been before – in it dwelt no good thing – and in it by it, Paul including ourselves as still being sold to sin.

So we find ourselves still doing the sinful things in spite of our conversion and regeneration and these look strange indeed and foreign to us. We see them in ourselves and know that we are guilty of them, but they seem to me, as they did to Paul as if another person other than myself is doing them. This is what makes Paul and many of us feel like a slave who is acting under foreign compulsion, a foreign power still having hold on him and on us.

- The unregenerate man possesses no such duality. He can never look at his evil deeds as not being really his own, his inner self has never been detached from them by a spiritual emancipation.
- Like Paul, we too feel that for not what we really will, this we do practice, but what we really hate, this we perform – our will now wills the Law.
- Our will is in harmony with God's Law but we fail, on the other hand, what I hate, what the Law condemns and what

my heart thus regards with aversion I perform instead of leaving it undone.
- These are simple elementary facts, the great anomaly, we constantly find with ourselves.

Sin and flesh in the unregenerate man are in the will. They fill and dominate his will completely. In the regenerate the spirit and not the flesh dominate the will, but not perfectly, not wholly. It is the spirit that wills the good and that hates any sin but the remnants of the old flesh that is still present ever and again interferes with the new will. It is this that makes the Christian sin in one way or another to his own grief and dismay.

A regenerate man's will agrees with God's Law, for it is what I do not will, that I perform. This is consent to the Law that it is "morally and spiritually excellent" and abominates the sin.

For as long as a man remains regenerate, and agrees with God's Law, (revealing of the sin and death) and continues in daily contrition (conversion, death to sin) and repentance (regeneration – death to the law) and the Holy Spirit (spiritual life in the will) "daily and richly God forgives all sins of such believers."

Our doing what we do not will but hate, these by consenting to the Law that condemns our own doing is and no doubt the duality.

There remains a sinful power that dwells in all believers, it does not possess and control us entirely, it is only lodged in us – it is still a foreign element that has not yet been dislodged and expelled. So here is **the truth** in a believer;
- He agrees with the Law.
- Not he in his own personality does these things that disagree with the Law, but the sin power still lodged in him.

- The sin power still existing in a believer is only in our flesh, which does not mean only in the physical body but in the old sinful nature that is still left in the regenerate man.
- The unregenerate man is all flesh, the old sinful nature and not merely so in part.
- The flesh still left in a believer is wholly bad and thus affords a place for the sin power to dwell.
- While flesh is still in us, its vileness and its violence are reduced to making us do only what is good-for-nothing morally and spiritually bad or base, thus opposed to the excellent Law and the excellence it requires. V20 Paul says: "not I, in my own person carry out this baseness, but the sin power that dwells in me, in my flesh."

So our entire wretched condition is summed up; willing the law in order to perform its excellence, we find the bad is still present, the baseness still present in our members – "I see another Law in my members, engaged in making me a war-captive by law of the sin, in my members." But this Law, this expression of "the sin" can do no more than "engage in campaigning against us and engage in making us war captive."

Conversion threw the Law of the sin power out of my mind and left this law only in the outer territory of my members. These members are still animated by flesh and the sin power thus operates in them, – meaning the sin power partly still has an inner hold in our souls and thus alone is able to make the animated members sin. Yet the real soul is freed, the spirit is joined to Christ and made dominant: the inner hold of the sin is only partial and gets weaker as sanctification proceeds and is left to show itself only in the lower part, its members. These are affected the more easily because they are surrounded by an outward sinful world, contact with which is inevitable and constant – V24.

Like Paul, this is the condition in which all believers find themselves, wretched is my body of sin, this is our mortal body – with the sin, still operating in its members by keeping up this disreputable ownership – for which we now need and cry for deliverance, not the riddance of this body as such, but the riddance of what makes our body with its members subject to death through the sin power that is still working in our bodily members.

A deliverance that is yet to come.

This can only be God, through Christ Jesus our Lord – the Mediator, His Person (Jesus) and His Office (Christ), His relation to us Christians (Our Lord) which has already been affected through Him and Him alone. This is our great assurance of hope and final deliverance; the liberty of glory of the children of God – the ransoming of our body. This goal will be reached in the next great Chapter Eight.

1. Through the Spirit leading us to live in the spirit until our mortal bodies shall at last be quickened and we are glorified.
2. And the Spirit leads us through tribulation in hope and nothing shall be able to prevent us from attaining that goal.

ROMANS CHAPTER 8:1-17
The Gospel is Our Spiritual Resurrection – (the Law of the Spirit)

The whole testimony of a believer (the evidence of spiritual life) is God's own work (God's Spirit) which consists of the following:
a) God's Creation and Deliverance
b) Redemption
c) The Resurrection

This God's Spirit changes human nature from fleshy to spiritual, through the Word by the operating power of Grace. So God's Spirit is the power of grace, the "*Causa efficiens*" or the effective cause of all that a Christian does:
1) The Law of the Spirit
2) It is the fulfilled Promise (believers are fully redeemed) – evidence of spiritual life
3) The Law of the Spirit Sanctifies

1) The law of the Spirit

What God's Spirit did for Paul and the believers in Rome, Paul can only describe his experience as a believer. What otherwise would be very difficult to explain, he does it in a perfectly brief manner of what God did for him and others through His own Law.

"The Law of the Spirit of life in Christ, this liberated me from the Law of sin and death."

- This "one law" is the expression of God's will which converts men from ungodliness (from sin and death) to a new life of godliness – the opposite of lawlessness, which is called flesh since it is the expression of the sin power which demands our disobedience to God's Law and of our obedience to the sin's lawlessness and unlawful demands. Now Paul freely adopts (loves) and obeys God's laws and sin's law is deposed and is able to disturb him only from outside through his members – the flesh still left in him.

So God's law i.e. the life in Christ superseded the Law of sin and death – this has taken place in the inner man – 7:32 in the mind or the spirit, and not as yet in his members, although that too is yet to come (ransoming of our bodies will come).

The Law of the Spirit liberated us from the Law of sin and death and our spiritual life constitutes our inner man who animates our body and moves our will to will the good law of God and not to will the base of things of the sin power.

- It is not God's law which changed but we changed, were made alive unto God and delight in His holy will as this is the voice in His Law.
- The sin – the sin power (the ungodliness) is always combined with death; death is always the companion of sin.
- This Law (general) – such as the Ten Commandments, cannot in itself liberate anyone, it cannot make any liberating work possible.
- It was God's use of a far higher means, the sending of His Son by whom He condemned the sin power itself in the very place where it exerted its full power, into the flesh so that we no longer need to live according to the flesh.

- There was no deficiency in the Law in securing the fulfillment of its righteous demands in us. All that the Law could and did secure was an aggravation of our lusts, nothing beyond stirring up and making alive the sin power in us thus producing "sin realization." So no deficiency in the Law, perfect in every way but the weakness of the medium in which the law worked was the flesh – man's sinful nature. And that rendered the Law weak, unable to accomplish the very thing to be accomplished: "our willing obedience."
- For our flesh can never be brought to obedience. All that could be done was to crucify it – (Galatians 5:24) and mortify it and get rid of it.
- Yet legalists and all governments of the world depend on law, still expect the Law to perform what is impossible for it to do, still think it is strong and mighty in the very thing in which it is utterly weak and helpless.
- Therefore God used another means – in the very flesh which rendered the Law so weak, God accomplished "sending His Son" in the likeness of flesh which rendered the law so weak, that it was impossible for it to accomplish the purpose to be attained.
- In the likeness of human flesh and in this way succeeded so that He condemned the whole sin power in the flesh of His son.
- Condemned the sin power so completely as to attain His great purpose.
- Our freely fulfilling what the Law requires so that we are now a people who walk not according to flesh, but according to spirit.
- It included the whole mission of the Son.
- In the likeness of human beings (our) flesh but His without sin.

- Jesus resembles men, all of whom had sinful flesh. He only resembled them because His flesh was not tainted with sin.
- The whole relation of Christ's mission was in relation to sin. As a power that removes sin – His birth, His preaching, His death and Resurrection demonstrated what life must be in Him, concerning sin, including His ability for atonement (death to sin) and our liberation (living not after flesh). Jesus (the Son) came into the world, among sinful flesh and revealed sin with "God's law." He became sin by being condemned by sinful flesh of men to death – thereby revealing the sin power in the most explicit manner.
- **Resurrected and now living: the greatest news of our ability to live not according to flesh – but in Him, with His Spirit, with all its hope for the resurrection – the very promise now fulfilled in His own body**.
- Jesus' whole mission is the righteous requirement of the Law i.e. what the Law has established as the right thing – which is walking after His Spirit, and not living after the flesh, as the unregenerate man, but in newness of life – This is indeed the true Creation – the New Life in Christ.

The difference:
- Those living after flesh – meaning conduct themselves in a fleshy fashion: consider and concern themselves with the interests, objects and the affairs of their unchanged old fleshy nature, to satisfy the cravings, the desires, the passions etc. of this nature. The enmity to God which is the output of flesh.
- In all their thinking they cannot rise higher to the other world – their fruit "is eternal death."

Those according to the Spirit: they mind the things of the Spirit, the entire new nature implanted in us in our justification; which is life and peace (the spiritual life).

2) It is the Fulfilled Promise – (Believers are fully Redeemed, Evidence of the spiritual Life.)

Christ redemption (the fulfilled promises) – was completed since the Spirit is the promise which we have now received i.e. our actual spiritual resurrection.

The flesh:
- Ungodliness is the evidence that there is no life in man except the spark that flickers and then finally is subjected to eternal condemnation.
- In flesh there is no life (i.e. that which lives on forever) and no peace.
- The unregenerate man cuts himself from the life because of his thoughts which are mainly earthly and this is the enmity to God.
- The enmity – for such a man does not subject himself to God's Spirit in contrition (guilty of sin) and faith in Christ, neither indeed is he able because every thought and product of the flesh rebels against God's law – God's Spirit.
- God and His Law are in its way and his fleshy body and soul rebels against God's Law. He wants them removed and as a result new laws and moral codes are invented.

Being fleshy is without excuse – God wants to remove it through His Spirit found in His Word which humanity has rejected. Flesh relies on intellect, science, capitalism, psychology etc. and of course law in general and the will of the flesh, all aptness, skill, capacity, aptitude to think, riches, culture, prosperity, fake religious ideas etc. cannot save man. It is only God's Spirit which enlightens. So flesh at large remains in the dark and in enmity to God.

The Christian spiritual life:
It is only the Spirit (God's law) which eradicates flesh through the realization of sin and death – the flesh is what man generally refers to as natural man – that which animates the body (the thoughts or mind) and the body itself.

- It is the Spirit of God that sets man free from flesh, to make it truly spiritual, to eradicate flesh and replace it with spiritual thoughts.
- In the new nature – (after conversion) God's own Spirit dwells in a Christian i.e. the heart or thoughts are prompted by the power which the Spirit supplies.
- The Spirit is equally God's and Christ's with all His saving power.
- Christ enters into our hearts with His Spirit and righteousness.
- With Christ in us, our new spirit – our new life – enters the body, although still subjected to sin by the flesh which still operates in our members – 7:23 as a result of contact with this world.
- So the Christian body is also doomed to death because it is still infected with sin, so passes through this death in order to be cleansed completely of this infection, and not in order to be abandoned to be lost.

So redemption is completed with two spiritual acts; first entrance – faith kindled and a new life immediately on conversion begins i.e. upon contrition and second on the last day of Christ's return.
- Christ is in us, His righteousness – the very spiritual power i.e. God's Spirit in us – is the very life principle, which continues as life eternal – the true redemption (Resurrection) at the last day of our Lord's return.

Although we see our Christian bodies are also marked with every ache and pain, every touch of sickness, but when we see Christ in us there we see "life" (not a flicker) never to end but pass on into glory.
- Christ's righteousness imputed to us becomes ours by justification through faith.
- Here now a distinction can be drawn between life – (spiritual life) as opposed to natural man or flesh.
- Before this life is ours – not a particle of sanctification, not a single good work is present but the moment life is kindled, these products and their evidences begin to appear. This life is always fed by the Word and not by its products – the more feeding on the Word, the more the strength in the spiritual life and the more the evidence.
- God looks at this real "life" which is in Christ and thus has no condemnation for those who are in Christ.
- The mortality and the death shall be swept out of our bodies together with the last trace of the flesh and of sin.

These mortal bodies shall be made alive by him who raised up Christ's body and shall be glorified like Christ's body. We are wholly redeemed and this is the promise fulfilled – the body as well as soul both redeemed. Having been created as embodied spirits, God will complete His work in us and will bring it to perfection also in our bodies. This is the constant promise of Jesus to all believers: "I will raise him up at the last day."

3) The Law of the Spirit Sanctifies

This is a reference to the Spirit which Paul and the Romans received, the new nature, and the life that God gave them and also gives to all believers.
- It is not like the spirit of the flesh which is slavery under sin and death, that is being under Law, which is of fear, that of the old life: which actually is real slavery.
- Our new life, although also referred to as enslavement but a world of difference. It is our free obedience to God which is voluntary, which comes from the heart, by our free choice and full liberty (i.e. freed from sin and death).
- This is the spirit of adoption, the language we understand well similar to the acquisition of a very willing company that was laden with sin and death as the debt but all of it met by the takeover company.
- Adoption refers to a state which describes God's operation in us which alters us inwardly. This act of God's operation is a divine act specifying the forensic act of justification, the wiping away, the condemnatory verdict of eternal death through our faith in Christ Jesus.

Further to this operation, God also gave us His own Spirit because he adopted us as sons – (Galatians 4:5) in which spirit now we can cry to him as the Father. Crying is the most appropriate word, as representing the deepest need in the heart for the divine power which removes sin and death and also continues with the gift of God's own Spirit which does not die but lives eternally.

As such are the sons of God alone whom God has rightly, (we may say) legally adopted. These alone have the spirit of adoption. It is with this spirit alone with which we put to death the doings of the body i.e. the flesh that is still in us, and to respond to the evil contacts made in this sinful world by our bodies.

- The body is the ally of the flesh and the spirit is the ally of God's Spirit in believers.
- With our spirit therefore we keep killing the evil deeds that the sin would like to bring about by misusing our eyes, ears, hands, feet, etc. All the desires of the old man (i.e. the flesh,) thus the combat is a mortal one. It is thus we say "the Holy Spirit" makes His temple in our hearts.

We are thus led by the Spirit and this Spirit of God is the agent who leads us. Thus being led involves obedience of faith, which involves our own spirit and the Holy Spirit which is the Written Word which is the Gospel – once someone has believed. Only in this way can we be led by the Spirit and these alone are God's sons and they alone befit a new life.

- Thus God's Spirit shapes the entire conduct as He leads God's sons. Here is a double proof of our new life in Christ, it is referred to as our obligation.
  1. Our spirit crying (or constantly realizing the greatest need of the salvation of our fleshy nature still remaining in us which subjects us also to physical death).

2. That of the Holy Spirit speaking through the Written Word, with the many assurances of our salvation on Christ's return.
- The testimony of the Spirit reaches us from the outside by men or the Word.
- Yet the Word may be misread, misunderstood, perverted etc. but the testimony remains what it is, in spite of the abuse to which it may be subjected. For that very reason, the Spirit's testimony is written and speaks in a mighty, cumulative voice and ever testifies against all perversions.

True children of God should have no difficulty in understanding it but alas who are the true children of God today?! So the assurance in the Word is in the hearts of God's children.

That testimony in their hearts is:
- God converts, justifies and adopts by the Word as the means of Grace and as an effective and operative power.
- Not until then does the Spirit use the testimony of the Word in a secondary function, namely as the assurance.

First the work wrought in us testifies as to what it is i.e. adoption and secondly, the Word that wrought this work testifies as to what it has wrought (redemption).
- Thus the two testify together. And their joint testimony is that we are "sons" as adopted persons, yeah! And children born in regeneration.
- Both are true, and together they join us to God so that we are surely debtors to him, to live not according to the flesh but according to the new spirit born in us.

The implication – if children, also heirs (Galatians 4:7 we are, if sons also heirs). Children by virtue of birth and sons by virtue of son-ship which rests on adoption; and our birth is effected in us by regeneration and this implies our inheritance – the promise.

Our inheritance is the Promise, co-heirs with Christ. He has already entered upon the inheritance in which we are now joined with him, namely His suffering. His suffering being vicarious while ours is not and cannot be. We suffer jointly with him because of our connection, with him for Christ's sake "in order that we may also be glorified with him. God will glorify us as He glorified Christ." That is – we are to become partakers of Christ's glory, body and soul, the soul when we die and body at the last day. Here is the complete motive not to live according to flesh, but for our joyful submission to spiritual guidance.

CHAPTER 8:18-39
Conforming to Christ's Suffering

The Gospel call is God's only power to save the world. To those who are saved again the Gospel is the common means for them to conform to Christ's suffering through:
1) God's loving providence (the called)
2) God's purpose (conformity) – Repentance through the call
3) Comfort – our actual confession and testimony

1) God's Loving Providence – (The Called)

Yes Adam's fall plunged the whole created world into vainness i.e. death and decay but the Christian hope is the very opposite of vainness; the eternal purpose for which all creation was created. Things look so confused at present: death and decay to all creation, injustices, wars, murders, natural disasters but amidst a world so sadly deranged, is the hand that makes all things work together for good to believers according to His eternal purpose – the realization of which is sure – the Christian hope and joy to our greatest comfort. This hand is God's Spirit which enables believers to realize the vainness of this world and at the same time the glorious hope.

The Christian suffering (his realization of vainness thus the suffering of the whole creature world into which we were

plunged by ourselves) and the glorious hope – God has bundled both the saved and the creature world into the one Christian hope.
- Even then, this whole suffering of vainness by believers and the created world; is nothing compared to the glory that is to be bestowed upon Christians as their inheritance.
- Now it is only hope and not yet in possession.
- So when this hope is fulfilled – then we shall have the unity of God's creation.
- Christ as the Head of all things in Heaven and earth – (Ephesians 1:10)
- God's Son will be supreme in all plus the true effectiveness of all creation for which it was created.

Vainness entered the world, which now also believers are subjected to but with one major difference i.e. with the Christian.
1) God extended grace (God's Spirit) to believers which they have embraced.
2) And this is the hope of glory planted into their hearts.

The rest of mankind has rejected this mighty restoration of God's Spirit which God has extended to all mankind. Great was the destruction but greater is the grace and restoration. The grace abounded and exceeded the destruction. So the children of God and the creation shall be liberated. Both are joined together in the great final emancipation but for the creation as only dependent on the children. As God's children, we have the promise of glory – (the eternal glory) the effulgence of perfection that never declines or ends, which belongs only to those who have embraced this grace or God's Spirit.
- Creatures together with children will be the Holy City now separated from the earth, shall end in union of both.

"Behold, I make all things new." The Christians now have the first fruits – the gift of the Holy Spirit – or spirit with which we are groaning.

The New Life
The major difference between a believer and a non-believer – is God's gift of the Spirit, the new life in a believer which is specified as spirit with small "s" or spirit with the Word as the source of this gift of spirit. With this spirit we are reborn – and it is only with this spirit by which Christians are able to recognize the full reality of this world's "vainness" and the "slavery of corruption" – on one hand, and on the other hand, the liberty of the glory awaiting us.

It is thus we groan:
- The ungodly cannot groan because they cannot attain this inwardness, they do not have this gift of Spirit.

Thus the godly ones continue in this groaning – by this spirit, the first fruit of assurance that in due time we shall receive the glory even that of the ransoming of our bodies and so we wait until the consummation arrives which is our great hope now in this life.
- When the body too will be raised from the dead and joined in glory to the soul and then there will be nothing beyond that which is still to be added.

The great object of our hope: the glory to be revealed; the liberty of the children: (the incorruption of the children).
- Who now walk by faith not by sight i.e. still in vainness.
- Heirs not yet in possession.
- Faith embraces salvation as it is present i.e. dead to sin and law as a result of the death and resurrection of Christ.

- And we have the hope which embraces salvation as what is yet in the future, the full liberty of glory. Hope rests on faith, and faith always bears hope with it.

Once the object of hope is seen, it ceases to be an object of hope, that is: once the glory hoped for is seen, the liberty which is the resurrection of our bodies is before our eyes – hope will have turned to realization.

During this period of waiting – the groaning remains and this is the activity of our gift of the spirit in our hearts which is translated into two activities;
- **The gift of spirit** in the hearts of the godly derives all confidence, support and strength from the **Holy Spirit** who is the Word.
- And with these two i.e. the spirit and the Spirit (Holy Spirit) we are able to wait long enough, even be prepared for any circumstance – even unto death.

It is this work of the two – spirit and the Spirit which is referred to as **God's loving providence** which takes care of those who have received the gift of spirit – i.e. those who are said to love God – who are contented in their great hope.
- For these alone: all things work together for good, all without exception, operate together to produce the good.

This (good) includes every kind of painful experience in Christian lives, all those that press groans from our lips and make us groan inwardly in unuttered and unutterable distress.
- The Old Testament's story of Joseph is a striking example of the mysterious and wonderful way in which God makes the evil done to us eventuate for our good.
- And so is the story of the persecution precipitated by Saul.

- It scattered the great congregation at Jerusalem to distant parts, which worked out for the good of the Church.

In fact this is what we find with our own experience when we look at the final beneficial outcome of our spiritual life, for the strangest and often the most contradictory occurrence seems to have cooperated to produce this unanticipated result. It is God's hand behind all our circumstances. It is God's love. Call it His providence. Salvation is the ultimate purpose of all good providences of God (or God's Love which consists of gifts of the spirit and the hope of glory). And this is what must lead us to wait upon the accordant intermediate purpose – waiting and accepting all eventualities – painful and unanticipated circumstances – "all good" names all these. So the purpose of "God's Love" is to transform believers into sons of God.

2) God's purpose – Conformity – Repentance through the Call

Those with God's love are the only ones who are loved by God. It is a reference to God's providence – those who have received the spirit and the hope. This love has nothing to do with being religious, dutiful in doing works of God or being charitable.
- It is not a certain pious behavior or moral requirement.
- The only one door open for God's love, only to those who by the divine means of grace have been made children of God with the spirit and hope.

God's love is His call according to a particular purpose, so "this call" tallies with God's purpose.
- It is this purpose which sets in motion the intended results to be attained.
- This purpose is the governing and normative power and is what is referred to as the "**The Gospel Call**." So when we think of the Gospel – it is a call with its intended purpose.
- This call and purpose is one and the same.

One faith: (immediate result) and final glory (the ultimate result – faith and glory)

So this Gospel call in its universality, identity and identical intent, it accords with God's purpose: – God's call according to purpose: an eternal advance divine knowledge that includes all that grace (the power of the Gospel call) would succeed in working in us – conforming.

The process of conformity through faith and grace.
- In John 10:14, Jesus "knows" certain persons as "My sheep" and these know Him as their "Shepherd."
- The divine power of grace is the very means to transform a man to the exact way of life God wants us to be, to restore us to His intended life and glory.

This is God's act of will; eternally fixed, settled and determined that those whom He already called i.e. recognized in His love, should be such as are conformed to the image of His Son.
- This conformity is set in motion by the power of grace through faith: faith and grace work together to bring about a reception of a form that is not a mere outward resemblance but one that is native to the essence or purpose or son-ship or God's children.

i. With faith and grace (purpose according to the call) we become copies of Christ, and this process is completed when we reach the state of glory: and then we shall be glorified with Him. Conformity is not attained until we reach the state of glory. The conformity to be attained – those who are called, God knows them in His Love;
ii. Which is to conform to the Son's image: which involved nothing but suffering of our Lord Jesus Christ.
iii. All have been called by His Love. God's love which involves the three: God the Father, the Son's suffering and the Holy Spirit which is the Word or the Gospel – which is the call of the Gospel which has gone out to all men to kindle faith in their hearts.
iv. This entire call involves God's own Spirit which is the entire Law which convicts all men with sin and death.
v. God's Spirit or the Law reveals and convicts the ungodliness in all men and *calls* all men to embrace God's means of salvation through faith in Christ – this is the repentance through the call – the conforming to the image of the Son.
vi. Those whom He has called out of ungodliness and have embraced Christ i.e. Christ's death to sin and Law, these also He has declared righteous on the basis of Christ's merits – pure grace pronounces a poor sinner free from guilt and sin and declares him righteous.
vii. And those whom He has declared righteous by means of grace – He also glorified (Holy Spirit's work through the Word and with God's gift of the Spirit inside our hearts with the hope of resurrection at the last day as Christ was also glorified), we too shall be glorified. These three are what the conforming to Christ's suffering mean i.e. being:
    a) Called
    b) Justified – glorified with His own Spirit
    c) Glorified – the hope of Resurrection

It is these three activities of God's Spirit which make us children born of the Spirit when faith is kindled and yet adopted as sons, given the promise, brethren of the First Born with an inheritance, the resurrection at the glorification day. All these three acts are done by God Himself; by means of the Spirit (or Holy Spirit). He knows them all by means of the Spirit. The rest of the world excludes itself, God did not exclude them but despite all that God could do they excluded themselves. Those He called, did only by means of acceptance of the call with its same power of grace to the rest.

viii. God's work is complete, complete from eternity to eternity, all these from the first saints to the last.
ix. From God's foreknowledge since time began to the glory of the saints when time shall be no more.

From these objective facts we reach the depth of our hearts – the subjective facts. The New life, a life that must be filled with the comfort that is beyond what is imaginable, far beyond the comforts of this earthly world which is not comfort at all – the actual liberation. The Spirit which set us free.

3) Comfort – our Actual Confession and Testimony

God's Spirit sets us free from all condemnation. Surely we Christians cannot stand and lament as though ours is a sad lot. No one can surely be against us if God is for us.

God began something at such a tremendous cost to Himself – spared not His Son (reference to Genesis 22:16) which scores the highest proof of Abraham's love when he offered his son also as a sacrifice.

x. God spared not His Son for the sake of miserable strange servants, debtors, (sinners) but endured even death just indeed to redeem that servant in substitution at a tremendous price.

xi. If He did that to His Son for us – surely if God is for us believers, who then can be against us in God's courtroom?
- Who then shall bring accusation against God's elect, when He is the Judge and the highest court in Heaven? Yet indeed we shall be accused often and shall even accuse ourselves, our conscience will often accuse us, but will it and others ever be successful against us, we who are God's elect in God's courtroom where the supreme judge sits?

xii. God will not listen to an accusation against people whom He elected for Himself in an absolute way; but the very reverse, that as a righteous and as declaring those righteous who are of faith in Jesus Christ – that is with God's Spirit. They are the elect according to God, the Father's foreknowledge because it is He who justifies: He is the Judge.
- Who then will condemn God's elect: some can bring accusations and condemn as well. If God will not condemn, others will condemn – suppose valid charges are ever brought or lodged against us. We are elect according to Grace, in God's love – foreknowledge.

xiii. All God's judgments, both acquittal and condemnation are by God Himself subjected to the whole universe of angels and of men for as to whether they are righteous – and in every way God's righteousness and justice must be and will be vindicated by the whole world. God's acquittal silences all and every condemnation by men and all others. In fact no person can condemn. Every person must assent to God's acquittal for the overwhelming reason that Christ Jesus has taken our part: He died, arose, sits at God's right hand and even intercedes for us.

- What Christ has done does not answer all condemnation, but it makes every condemnation of any person impossible. Before Him who died in obedience even to death on the Cross every knee will bow and every tongue confess that He is, indeed the Savior Lord (Philippians 2:10–11).

xiv. So sufficient was His sacrificial death as to make impossible any voice of condemnation against them (the believers).

- Another set of danger against God's elect, not with judicial assaults but with direct assaults in order to separate us from God's saving love. But we know that nothing and absolutely nothing can separate us from the love of Christ.

xv. Tribulations, anguish, persecution, hunger, nakedness, perils at sea, murder or even death etc. we know that nothing of the kind can separate us from God's love.

Sometimes we may physically feel the pangs of pain from the evils of this world and even be compelled to taste the evils mentioned above, at times these overwhelm our barks as the disciples on the Sea of Galilee while Jesus was asleep – these afflictions appear like a gulf that separates us from Him.

xvi. Nothing and absolutely nothing of any kind can sunder the tie of faith that connects us with the love of Christ. The elect cannot lose their faith; His love reaches out to save them in every situation. Should one ever lose his faith, His love reaches out still to save them.

xvii. Painful things may shake the tie of faith, but most often the loss of faith is through the cunning lies and deceit that are handed out as real faith.

Sword, hunger, hatred, poverty, sickness; etc. when they come upon us, they do not look like tender caresses of love; they look as though God has abandoned us, as though these were blows of wrath.

xviii. This is not a sign that God has abandoned us, but a sign for the very opposite, in tribulation we should rejoice; conquer them through Him who loved us – the supreme act of love when He died for us. Christ's love constitutes the ultimate means by which we conquer.

xix. With it we settle every debt that afflictions would arouse – so in the same manner we too like Paul arrive at our personal confession and testimony.

Our own conviction wrought in us by God's love – the gift of the Spirit testifies to us that nothing in this world can stop God's love from reaching and holding us, so great is this love. The certainty of this love should bring this reality automatically in our hearts, that:

"Nothing can separate us" from His Love and this conviction has nothing to do with our own doing. Of course Judas separated Himself from God's love, so others will, personal reasoning, thoughts, etc. cannot take one far. The Holy Trinity (the Word) God the Father, God the Son and God the Holy Spirit, directs all men to Christ, as the Book of Life, in whom we should seek eternal election of the Father.

xx. This had been decided from eternity, that whom He would save, He would save through Christ.

This means no condition of my existence, whatever death or life, no being whether they be angels or men, nothing in time, whether present or in future, nothing in the way of power or forces, nothing in space, or depth; in fact, nothing in all creation, no matter what it may be called, not only shall not, but even cannot separate us (believers) from God's saving love by placing a barrier between God's love and believers so that it cannot reach them.

This love of God which is also the same as Jesus' love climaxed in connection with the death of the Son. The result of which is our justification through faith and our hope in glory which is yet to come at the day of Our Lord's return – behold the gift of the Spirit.

ROMANS CHAPTER 9:1-33
God's Sovereignty and power

God is the supreme power in this whole vast universe and there is no other power above him. His sovereignty extends to all His creation most importantly to mankind. God's authority over man is most amazing. It consists of His counsel or guidance by simply extending favor to man and also His omnipotence when His favors are rejected. The whole purpose of His sovereignty over the world is to restore man to God's intended purpose of creation – eternal life by simply extending favors. These favors are everything that men need for this restoration when they find those who lost everything. These favors include:

1) God's great plan of Salvation – the Seed of Israel
2) Mercy for wretchedness
3) Long Suffering (His patience with the vessels of wrath)

1) God's Great Plan of Salvation – God's counsel (the Seed of Israel)

All God's authority works in this world by extending favor to man. God's favor first came to man whom He created in His image, giving him eternal life. God in His counsel (favor) determined to restore man by revealing Himself to Abraham yet again with undeserved favor – the promise of salvation. This promise of salvation through Abraham was simply to be accepted as the sweetest promise in Abraham's ears. This made Abraham carry out all God's own counsel (Word) in trust, knowing that they would lead to salvation as God's promise. Thus through God's extension of favor Abraham found himself in Egypt, where his offspring grew numerous into the twelve tribes of the Jews. There in Egypt they were to be isolated from the idolatry and paganism of the Gentile tribes, while they waited for the promise God made to their Father Abraham.

Unfortunately few of the Jewish people remained true to the Promise and those alone who remained true to the promise, were referred to as the Israelites – a title which goes back to Jacob whose name God had changed to Israel (the contender with God) in honor of his prevailing faith in the Promise given to Abraham and the patriarchs. To all those who remained in the faith of Abraham, God gave all spiritual gifts promised. God adopted them as His sons and they were thus given the theocratic name Israelites – a reference to the Fathers. "Israel was my son whom I called out of Egypt." (Hosea 11:1) "My son, firstborn." (Exodus 4:22) "A peculiar treasure unto me above all people." (Exodus 19:5) etc. To these alone God advanced the progressive covenants. Bestowed on Israel was the glory (the Kebod Yahweh) their Jehovah during their sojourn to the Promised Land.

- The Pillar of cloud by day and fire by night guided them.
- The laws on Mount Sinai (the law to reveal their sin and the tabernacle to prefigure the sacrifice to come).
- "The cultus" – the regulation of Israelites' worship of the true God.

All the above prefigured the Promise pertaining to the Messiah and to the New Covenant (Testament).

The rest of the Jewish people were also given the same highest prerogative of Israelites, the highest of them all was God's Son who came from Israel according to His human nature – but these undeserved gifts were rejected.
- This Christ is the very divine gift promised, the Savior among themselves to save them from sin and death by restoring godliness into their hearts by faith; but they rejected both these undeserved gifts of the Savior – (The Promise).

What made Paul's grief so poignant is the fact that God should have favored the Jews so highly with the highest spiritual blessing of Christ (grace). An Israelite according to the flesh, Lord of all – with all the miracles proving His saving grace but they still rejected him. They could not trust him as the Savior, the permanent sacrifice for their sins and the promise for their resurrection.
- This is the very same (God's counsel) gift which men of this world have rejected by not putting their trust in the person of Christ.

From the very beginning God operated with faith and this implied reception of the gift by faith only. Only those who believe in the Promise of Christ are the children – the true Israelites. The scriptural term Israel therefore does not refer to the physical descendants of what we now refer to as Israel i.e. Israel does not refer to all descendants of Abraham, and a specific territorial area, but to only those who remained in the faith of Abraham. So also the seed does not refer to Abraham's physical children nor the children of flesh but spiritual children, God's children, the children of the promise – those of faith in Christ.

So it follows, all those derived from the physical territorial Israel, not all of them are Israel or seed of Abraham in the spiritual sense. And as such, spiritual children of the Promise derived from Israel or the seed of Abraham have the true character which God must recognize. This is the covenant of faith. Those who receive the promise by faith alone have the following characteristics:
1) Only these have been "called."
2) And only these God acknowledges to be the spiritual seed and the true Israel.
   - So Christ was the promised gift in the Covenant, who would save not only the patriarchs but the whole world.
   - He would also **regulate the souls of men by kindling faith** into the heart of every individual. And also ensure the gift of the New Life which God anchored in this Covenant in the three patriarchs.

So Abraham is to have the seed (the promise, the Savior to come) in connection with Isaac, even as Jacob was to be the third. With these three patriarchs, God would establish the only means of salvation (Christ) through faith in the word. Abraham put all his faith in the Promises of Christ, the same faith was established in Isaac, in Jacob and then finally in connection with the twelve patriarchs, the sons of Jacob and then the covenant would be open to others who with the same faith in the promise of the Savior would become the seed or the true Israelites.
- All would enter it by faith (the called).
- All would be acknowledged by God as the seed of Abraham as having been saved by the same faith in Christ as their fathers.

The line of those with the same faith would go through Judah and then on and on until we reach David and eventually Jesus the Seed – the promised Savior would be born. With Him the old covenant and its line of bearers ends because it has attained its goal of the promised Savior.

The covenant which god made to Abraham, or the three patriarchs is the blessed promise of the covenant of grace which has two sides:
i) The Promise of the Seed or Christ with His work fulfilled.
ii) The recipients of the **Grace, Israelites** with their faith in Christ.

So the Seed and Israelites – the two words which complete the fundamental meaning of God's great plan of salvation – **God's supreme authority and power having attained its goal.** So as such Israelites, God reckons them children of the Promise – the spiritual seed. Children of the Promise is the counterpart of the opposite of the flesh – physical descendants.

The promise is the source and origin of children of God. The covenant promise is the Gospel or Christ's promise which brings forth children of God by faith and by faith alone. God's authority and power worked only to this end among the Jewish people.
- We are children of the promise (Grace) when this promise leads us to believe what it promises.
- Every promise is to be believed so that what it extends is actually accepted and it is true in the highest degree with regard to this promise of the Savior.

It reaches out to all men in order to kindle faith in all of them. This promise does not exclude any man from the very promise itself, the Gospel which is Christ. The promise extends to all including the Gentiles and it is God's objective means which require the correlative subjective means which is faith.

2) Mercy for Wretchedness

First, this mercy is evidenced in the judgment which men force God to bring down on them. God disregards works of any kind when bestowing His great promises. This may lead anyone to think of something like injustice. All Christians would repudiate the thought. Therefore, righteousness (justice) belongs to the very nature of God. To be merciful is to show grace and what it involves.

Mercy is the supreme purpose of God's counsel who governs all affairs of the world whether man is aware of this or not. The great patriarchs, the progenitors of the chosen people consisted of three patriarchs. God desired and used only three and His purpose was to save.

- None of them had anything that God could use, no works or merit which God could use to restore man to his original purpose. No principle He could use.

The choice lay between two only; one of pure grace or one based on meritorious works and no such works could be found among them or in any other person.

"I will have mercy on whomever I will have mercy" meaning I will not demand works for no man is ever able to furnish God with any good works.

- It was utterly hopeless to try to fill any of the three patriarchal places by meritorious works.
- Such competition of this sort, all competitors had to fail.
- Only one way was open – the purpose according to election – the position had to be awarded solely by a call or an appointment that came from God – (the extending of mercy).
- In making this call, God would have to disregard all works and depend only on Himself – **His grace making the choice.**
- Thus it came about: so the call came to Rebecca, not by order of birth, too slight a matter to turn his appointment either way.
- By telling Rebecca, God also told Isaac and thus also told the twins Esau and Jacob when they grew up.
- This was a gracious promise for all of them, the brother of Esau to be the third representative covenant bearer (the seed) or progenitor of **the chosen nation – Israel.**

Esau's nation being stronger than Jacob's and yet God chose the weaker as the covenant bearer (1Corinthians 1:27 and 2Corinthians 12:10) the covenant of promise and faith.
- Jacob was the third patriarch, Esau was thus the inferior.
- As in Isaac's seed was to be called for Abraham so also in Jacob.
- Esau had the covenant in the twin brother (i.e. the salvation, which is pure gracious promise) even as Jesus says salvation is for the Jews.

So in Malachi 1:2–3 "Jacob I treated with an act of love but Esau with an act of hate" (God's wrath). This perfectly illustrates how the Israelites got all the gifts (adoption, covenants, etc.)

- All were pure gratuitous gifts of love. The Jews should have recognized what God had done for them with His grace and His gratuitous promise which would save all of them.
- They should have each of them become children of the promise.
- They did nothing of the kind, they did the exact opposite, they refused faith, they became obdurate in unbelief, grew presumptuous and outrageous.

Extending mercy – emanates from Him who offers mercy.
- Mercy and works exclude each other.
- Everything that was extended to the patriarchs must be viewed in reference to the idea of mercy i.e. wretchedness and undeserving.
- When viewed as extending to Israelites, they are referred to as pure mercy for adoption, the covenants, the giving of the Law, the fathers and of whom concerning the flesh and Christ came.

True sovereignty in connection with God's mercy and pity is that God extends it to whomever He wills, unhampered, unrestricted by limits that men may set up.
- Undisturbed by charges of injustice that men's foolish reasoning may prefer.
- In God's blessed sovereignty He shapes what He will so that the sweet purpose of mercy and pity will be attained to the utmost among men.

To what extent does God's mercy go? Far beyond what men would think impossible, and thus there is no sovereignty that restricts mercy and pity – that is, in God there is no sovereignty that places mercilessness and pitilessness for all the rest beside **mercy and pity for a few. Mercy and still more, pity are called out by the wretched condition of those who have lost everything and plunged into woe.** There is only the sovereignty that overthrows restriction such as men think should be set up by works of theirs or by secret eternal decrees of God.

What this means:
When God showered the streams of mercy on Israel, He inaugurated the plan to send Christ and salvation for all nations of the world – Genesis 18:18. This vast unrestricted mercy was the purpose and substance of the first covenant with Abraham.

- God also anchored the same plan in the three patriarchs which started with Abraham, not for themselves but for all those to whom this covenant could possibly extend.
- Ishmael and Esau had the covenant, hence even the sign of circumcision (Genesis 17:26) but rejected it.
- The sovereign design of mercy and His pity extended to the utmost, and in this extension, not as one of a man willing, exerting as running or not running.
- Mercy and pity are directed towards the wretched who have lost everything and have no power to run or even to will, far removed, too, is the thought of restriction as though if men will ever so earnestly, run ever so tremendously. All is in vain if they are not among the elect. The prize of God's mercy and pity would not be accorded him. They remain under God's merciless and pitiless judgment of damnation. Mercy is for God alone, His seeing our utter helplessness, wretchedness and misery and thus letting His heart go out to them in mercy. They are directed towards the wretched and the lost who have no power

to run or even will. Those who reject them remain under God's merciless, pitiless judgment of damnation. Our woeful state and nothing else in us or done by us moves him. Oh, that we would understand mercy aright, we would recognize that it is all of him that has mercy, we would then in gratitude drink in that pure, sweet mercy.
- Our woeful state and nothing else in us or done by us moved Him but mercy alone.

3) God's long suffering (His Patience with Vessels of Wrath)

This answers the question; why doesn't God destroy all the wicked people in this world? How God's promises and mercies are carried out we see Pharaoh and Moses belonging together.
- Moses the mediator of the initial fulfillment of the promises of the patriarchs and the tyrant who sought to block this initial fulfillment.
- The wickedness of this tyrant revealed to the whole world, in all generations, the sovereign power and glory of the Name which carries all God's promises, mercy and pity in the covenant which gave Christ and salvation to the world.
- The longsuffering is itself mercy. It was the divine purpose of raising Pharaoh to Egypt's throne, that God might show forth His power through him.
- The whole world to this day has witnessed with what mighty power God carried out His plan of mercy among His people who were being crushed and ground to noth-

ing by the fierce tyrant. This is not mere omnipotence or omnipotence set over and against mercy but omnipotence serving mercy.
- God's omnipotent power alone carried out the promises and mercy in Israel's deliverance from Egypt.
- The Lord rules even in the midst of His enemies (Psalms 110:2). You and I might have ended things with one or two plagues but God sent ten. The use God made of this wicked man reveals how His omnipotence carries through its plans.
- This Omnipotence in the case of Pharaoh enabled God's Name to be published abroad. Name **means revelation of who and what God really is in love, mercy, grace and saving power** – a perfect definition for God's Word or the sovereignty of God.
- The publication of the Name, filled with the Gospel of mercy, mightily carried out in all the earth – it resounds to this day in the darkest corners of the continent of Africa and many other parts of the world.
- To this day the Jews celebrate the Passover which keeps publishing the Exodus.
- But the Christians and the Christian Church publish the Name as it was connected with the Exodus and with all to which the Exodus was to lead to, in all the earth – and that is the salvation of the world.

So God – on whom He wills, He has mercy – but men exclude themselves by first hardening themselves against God's mercy. And then God's mercy closes the door gradually and God is ready to open it wide again at the least show of repentance in answer to His mercy; and not until all the warnings of gradual closing are utterly in vain, does the door sink regretfully into its lock.

It was only after the seventh plague that God started the hardening of Pharaoh's heart. Pharaoh wanted none of this mercy for himself. For the Jews – all mercy was covenanted to be theirs, but they did not only refuse it, but also crucified Christ and intended to prevent all other men from receiving this mercy too – (Mathew 23:13). God certainly carries out His resolutions and no man is able to resist them. But the victims of God's counsel (such as Pharaoh and the Jews) cannot possibly be blamed on God who resolved that counsel.

- Many presumptuously and arrogantly blame or doubt the justice of God's ways.
- Our little logic takes God to task, answering back to God, contradicting Him; the arrogance which levels itself with God, which actually is man's inability to see the infinite and the perfect will of God.

It is the case of a vessel blaming a potter, and so was the lump; Moses and Pharaoh; the believing and the obdurate Jews were of the same clay. We must always be able to see the immensity of His mercy and the intense purpose to make known His riches to men by living examples in order to draw them to this mercy. Why not destroy the wicked straight away? The astounding fact is that God bears with the wicked in order to advertise His mercy the more, in order to save men from hardening. God has the will to strike them down for judgment immediately yet He delays this in the interest of grace. Foolish men may think otherwise, God is willing to run that risk.

- Displaying His grace is supreme.
- Warnings and winning those who would be saved.
- There is mercy even in God's wrath and the power visited on the wicked. The longsuffering – delays the wrath to be visited on the wicked because of His immense purpose.

And this is the triumph of God's mercy. He who excises such mercy, He does to such a degree and to such an extent that no one can find fault with Him when He judicially hardens those who adamantly reject or be against such mercy.

Two examples of the tragic obduracy of the bulk of the Jews
a) God showed His wrath – the ten tribes of the northern kingdom who were completely idolatrous, a non-people – were deported and swallowed up and lost identity – thus was the wrath or omnipotence of God; but this was not to be the end of the story.
   - With God's promise to the spiritual children of Abraham – this intermixture with the Gentiles was not to be the end of the story. The Gospel finally reached the ends of the earth.

Above all that, what God does with vessels of wrath, rises to His purpose regarding vessels of mercy;
"They will at last be called" sons of the living God.
The true Israel shall indeed be saved, become numerous as indeed the sands of the sea.
God restrained His wrath so that the seed was left. The purpose of God's mercy is to kindle faith, to be received and retained by faith. All mercy is of the same nature, to be received by the faith it awakens and that faith trusts nothing else.
The bad thing about worldly political systems is that they put their trust in materialism and the legal system themselves, instead of the worship of the True God who declares a man righteous for Christ's sake. Faith obligates God to grant His mercies while works obligate God to recognize our obligations where there is none – thus both Jews and many Gentiles have stumbled on the rock thus crushing their brains out.

b) In the case of the hardened ruler – the whole world got to hear and not only the wrath and power but much more, the riches of His glory on vessels of mercy.
   - Judgment upon Judas was delayed, for Jesus' warning, but his treachery served only to work out Christ's redemption.
   - The Jews fit for destruction were left for 40 years, during which time, His mercy built up the Church out of the Jews and the Gentiles.

Longsuffering:
God still bears with the obdurate ones for the same purpose. The purpose of His longsuffering is in order to make known His riches of glory (His love, grace, mercy) on vessels of wrath in order to awaken faith.
i) Who would have known about God's mercy towards Israel if God had struck down Pharaoh at the first day when Moses demanded his release?
ii) Who would have known about God's mercy towards the Church that was made up of the Jews and Gentiles if God had destroyed the Jewish nation, when Herod killed John the Baptist, or when the Sanhedrin first plotted Jesus' death?

So we have vessels of mercy and vessels of wrath i.e. fitted for destruction – the devil fitted them and the vessels of mercy which God made ready in advance for glory, to be received in glory in heaven. God could have taken the vessels away but wants to let the world know the glory of His mercy which is resting on them. These vessels are the very purpose of God's omnipotent power.

ROMANS CHAPTER 10: 1-21
The Supremacy of God

We live in a world divided up by super powers, with each group with its own area of influence and all are gearing up for World War III. Main super powers include USA, Russia and China with threats from Iran, Syria and North Korea. They all have nuclear weapons enough to destroy the world over many times. All aim at achieving the supremacy by their own means and laws, the thing that is utterly impossible. WW III may be one which cannot be won by an individual and even then, why war and what is the purpose? What is the answer to this looming doom? It is only God's Word which gives the water-tight answers to these disturbing developments. The solutions are found in Chapter 10 of Romans and these include:
1) One God, One Nation, One Rule of Righteousness
2) His Lordship
3) The utterance of faith

1) One God, One Nation, One Rule
(The Law divides, the Gospel Unites)

Abraham in his heart was totally convinced that he could not uphold the righteous demands of God's Law and so were the Patriarchs.

- He also knew that anything concerning the quality of righteousness for he himself could only come from God, simply as a gift to be received by faith alone; and so did the Patriarchs.
- They (the Patriarchs) further understood very well that through God's Law, sin in them was revealed, and they were worthy of eternal death except for God's quality of Grace and mercy, where there was only unworthiness and wretchedness.

This is where the rest of the Jews and the rest of the world have stumbled as regards the Word or God's utterance which consists of; first of the Law which reveals sin with its penalty of eternal death and secondly the Gospel of faith with its gift of God's righteousness. The Word communicating the Law or command is what the Jews and the world wrongly took into their hearts as the righteousness demanded by our Maker – God.
- It is this misunderstanding of the Law which divides up nations, causes enmity and leads to death.

And as a result of Law being their motivation, the Jews burned with excessive zeal which also Paul himself testifies as he once burned with (Acts 8:1).
- As a result of the commandment, they hated the worship of idolatry and reverence for the Temple, with their tithes and with all outward observance of the Law, etc., the same zeal which burns in the majority of all religious groups today with different ways of worship – and some have put Christ out of their Churches by replacing the Gospel of faith with the prosperity Gospel. All these groups do different things under the zeal of their own built up laws as the Jews

also burned with the Law of Moses. Their zeal (as a result of law) is not according to knowledge that comprehends, much of it is motivated by religious laws, qualifications, sincerity and nothing on the substance that sincerity includes. All that is being done and practiced sedulously is without the true knowledge that comprehends or understands the truth in the Word.
- Errors with fanatical zeal are accepted as truth or sincerity and are devoid of God's intended plan of salvation which was anchored in the Patriarchs, the righteousness of the Gospel of faith.

God's righteousness consists of Christ and not without the personal appropriation by faith.

Not to know this righteousness does not mean to be entirely ignorant of it but most of the time, it is simply rejected, refusal to accept it as the only righteousness and instead men establish their own righteousness by engaging in creating it by Law and works.

There is only one other righteousness – which men are ever seeking, and pursuing, but not catching up with (Romans 9:31.) This righteousness if it was attained would emanate solely from men themselves. This one comes from the Law, the righteousness of works. Righteousness as a result of Law is very different from that which arises from the Gospel faith. The two are mutually exclusive. The Jews did not subject themselves to the righteousness of faith which is wrought in us by God through His Gospel faith, and is never wrought in us by ourselves. And only this righteousness eliminates enmity and divisions. It eliminates wars and enables us to recognize God as supreme.

This righteousness is through Christ alone and our faith in Him. For the end of the Law is Christ for everyone believing.

The status of righteousness does not depend on Law, effort, achievement of ours, measuring up to some Law – it is wholly a matter of believing or faith in Christ. The quality of righteousness from Law as emphasized in V5; Law requires perfect doing. Moses himself, a man whom God gave the great Jewish code of law talks about its quality: the man who did the things of Law shall live in them – meaning if there was such a man, him alone shall live – which implies there has never been any such man.

- Living in them means continuing without a break and would reach perfect completion, meaning all of them perfectly and completely done. A single break or omission in the many things to be done, is fatal.

Man in his sinful condition, right from the start there is no chance to apply Law, no hope to achieve such righteousness by doing Law except only Pharisaic blindness (John 9:40–41). The entire Jewish legal system with all its sacrifices for sin, proclaimed that no man could do law and thus gain righteousness and life from fulfilling the Law. This is the doctrine of Law, the Jews knew it, hence their constant sacrifices – we too (Christians) ought to know it. Further still; both the Law and the Gospel come to us through the Word. On this score, Law and the Gospel do not differ – although they are opposites in all other respects, especially as regards our obtaining righteousness by them as the means. But their different nature makes the Word differ when it brings them (i.e. Law or Gospel).

- In the case of the Law or (Commandment) the Word bringing it can only command "that thou mayest do it" (Deut. 30:14).
- While in the case of the Gospel the Word bringing the Gospel righteousness is one that we may only believe without any doing on our part because:

- Christ came down from Heaven and actually brought us God's own righteousness to be received from Christ by faith.
- It is this very God's righteousness which calls out to us not to ask with discouraged hearts, who will ascend up or descend down to bring righteousness, etc.
- This God's righteousness has already been purchased and won for us by Christ.
- It is here for us in the Gospel Word and through the Word in every believers' mouth and heart, but in a more blessed way: It does not ask us first to do commandment in the Word, but only to believe and allow God to give us Christ's blood and righteousness by our believing in Him.

It is this very Gospel Word which is full of Christ and His righteousness which aims at, produces, and fills with faith. God brought this righteousness by sending His Son from Heaven, by raising Him from the dead (the abyss – His earthly work) and God embodied it in the Word by means of which we have it in our hearts by faith. The Jews heard the Word but scorned what it brought and acted like people who would climb up to Heaven and down into the Abyss and thus get righteousness for themselves – i.e. to do what the commandments demanded.

- All has been done, no effort of ours is needed, and these needs would be impossible ones as going up into Heaven and going down into the Abyss, as bringing Christ down and bringing Him up when, lo, in the very words once used regarding the commandment (Law) we have the truth.

"Nigh to thee is the utterance concerning the faith" – the personal justifying faith, the contents of which is Christ – the very righteousness which is ours through faith. Our righteousness is to be believing hearts and we are to use the Law rightly for daily contrition and repentance for our hearts guide to serve God rightly. The Word therefore concerning the law is not indeed aimed at attaining such righteousness.

But the **Gospel Word** when it is uttered and preached, has ever brought God's righteousness, placed it right into the "mouths" of the hearer, to talk about it, discuss it, make it their own, confess it, write into their heart, to hold it there by faith. The Word uttered is the great medium: and being the Gospel Word and not command, **FAITH** is its reception, and unbelief is its rejection. Since the medium of God's righteousness, the uttered Word, is the same as Law, it should have been easier for us all to receive the Gospel as to receive the Law. Easier, in fact, because the Gospel is pure gift. But we have received even the **Law outwardly** and not in the heart and closed our hearts obdurately against the Gospel Word with its gift of righteousness. This righteousness would have produced One Nation – Israel, One faith, one confession and One Church.

2) God's Lordship (Supremacy of God)

The establishment of the Lordship of Christ with His gift of righteousness is the confession of God the Almighty as supreme in our hearts. The Divine Word placed both commandment (Law) into mouth and into the heart and so the same Word did this with the Gospel.
- placed into the mouth as thy confession
- and into the heart as thy faith

This confession voices faith, and what is voiced is faith in Jesus as Lord i.e. what He is in our hearts as the exalted Savior, Mediator, whom we trust, worship and obey, the very contents of the Gospel.

- He is the very one "that God raised from the dead," thereby establishing Him as "both Lord and Christ." His resurrection crowned the work of salvation, revealed and forever sealed the efficacy of all that Christ had done, especially the full atoning power of His death, so that, if thou shalt so confess and believe "thou shalt be saved."

But see what the Law states: Moses says in V5 "that he that does it… shall live," meaning shall not lose life, shall not die, shall go on living as never having committed a sin – a hopeless promise for the sinner!

"Shall be saved" connotes the fact that we have sinned and are thus doomed as being dead in sins: and the Gospel utterance declares that the confession and the believing sinner shall be rescued and put into permanent safety by the Divine Savior – our Lord. This is the eternal joy of a sinner.

The Word of the Gospel aims at faith in the heart and at confession by the mouth, and true faith always speaks out in confession – the double result is "righteousness" and "salvation." The instant a sinner believes, righteousness results i.e. the divine verdict that for Christ's sake this believing sinner is accounted righteous. This is justification by faith alone. Also to be justified is to be saved. In (John 3:15–16) believing at once secures life eternal i.e. salvation, this is the deliverance that transfers into Heaven. All legalistic ideas must be dropped and become like anyone believing, whether Jew or Gentile, or Greek, barbarian; as long as it is the **Gospel Word** which has brought about the confessing faith and nothing but this faith.

There is absolutely no distinction since the same One is "Lord of all" namely Jesus whom the Word leads us to trust and to confess as Lord – V9. The universality lies in the means of grace employed by God – to everyone believing.

The same Lord of all beings "is rich toward all those calling upon Him." The wealth of His saving grace and merits is never wearied or exhausted.

The Word is the Name:
To call upon Him for mercy is faith and confessing Him is one and the same act. The main confession which we make of Jesus **as Lord** is thus **to call** upon Him.

(Joel 2:32) "Everyone whoever **shall call on the Name** (Yahweh) of the Lord shall be saved." The Name which always signifies the revelation of God, of the Trinity, of Christ. The Name is the means by which God comes to us, by which we have Him, without which we cannot reach Him.

The Word is His Name. The Name is intended for faith and confession, for justification and salvation. There is salvation in no other Name. We can now see what the Word does, it is the only means for bestowing God's righteousness upon sinners who could obtain righteousness by no other way but the Word.

And this Word as the means for making this righteousness ours involved several links in the chain. In the first place, the Word makes no distinction between rich or poor, Jew or Gentile, white or black; for each and every one, it is the same Word to give any and every one the righteousness and it is equally easy for anyone.

But how will anyone ever call upon one in whom he has no faith or confidence? This is a general concept: No one can call upon anyone in whom he has no faith or confidence. This reveals the fakeness in many Christians who have not come to the true knowledge of God through Christ. So if a sinner is to call for God's mercy, He must have faith implanted in him. So every call for mercy and grace involves faith. But then another dilemma: how will anyone believe in a person whom he has not heard, has had no contact or have no confidence? Confidence in a man is wrought in only one way: the man himself must awaken it in us.

How can we have such confidence in God?
To see His deeds is not different from hearing Him, for them to speak. There are two ways of hearing a person: when he himself speaks in his own person as Jesus spoke when He was on earth, and when he sends a herald to utter his message as Jesus sent His Apostles as heralds.

- These heralds announced no word more or less than he is bidden to announce and alters and changes nothing.
- He merely lends his voice to His Master who often is also present in person. This the Apostles were to do, and they did it, and their message still rings through the world.
- This also the prophets before the apostles did, and often with the direct preamble: "Thus saith the Lord." "He that heareth you heareth me, and he that despiseth you, despiseth Him that sent me." (Luke 10:16)

Applied to many who preach today, this means they are supposed to be Christ's heralds through whom men hear Christ Himself, only when we transmit His Word exactly as He has commanded it to us.

But before they can herald – one more link or qualification: they must be commissioned. He alone is a herald who is not only sent and commissioned but who with the commissioning he presents the Word as the great means of grace, for working confessing faith unto righteousness. This Word, being preached: with the heart it is believed, with the mouth confessed – many are calling upon the Lord, and so righteousness and salvation are being received without distinction between Jew and Greek. This is the supremacy of God who is above all earthly powers and he alone can save from sin and death.

It is this fact (the chain) that makes the dusty feet of the heralds beautiful of those telling as glad news "good things." Near to thee is the Word – the Gospel Word that is God's means of salvation. "Go," cried Jesus, "disciple all nations, and with that commission speeded the feet of His heralds." Such were the feet of Paul when he wrote those Epistles.

It is this utterance which makes the wise simple, that removes all barriers between rich and poor, educated and uneducated, black or white, Jew or Gentile – all would be in one Church under one leadership God the supreme with His gift of righteousness.

3) The Utterance of Faith

It is no longer only Jewish unbelief, but unbelief of the whole world – which has rejected the righteousness which comes to us all by the gracious means of the Word, its reception thus being only by faith. In fact in many churches, the word **faith** is no longer the central doctrine or truth in the Scripture which is expounded but the new gospel of this generation.

The Word calls us to come only as poor, lost sinners, and only by hearing and believing; to be declared righteous, but such call has aroused the most violent silent opposition, not only in the Jewish world at that time, but also in all generations including the present one.

This rejection of God's righteousness through faith is the rejection of the Gospel Word as a result of the non-commissioned preachers who go about preaching day in day out, in all places of the world. This rejection has been the same opposition which existed 800 years before Christ's time in (Isaiah 53:1) and also voiced by Stephen with fearful indictment (Acts 7:51). Only in this sense is Isaiah's prophetic word relevant to our day as we too fill up the measure of the "Jewish fathers" recorded in Matthew 23:31–32. "They are the children of them which killed the prophets."

Few believed what was heard in Isaiah's time, the prophets', Stephen and Paul's time and even at the present time. Central to hearing is what is to be heard: namely the Gospel Word (Isaiah 40–64.)

The faith must be the result of what one is made to hear and this thing (the Gospel) is mediated by Christ's own uttered Word. Hearing is very well defined. It is not the mere act of hearing, but out of what is heard, namely the Gospel itself, this brings about the saving faith which brings righteousness and salvation – V6. Only the Gospel faith is what men must be made to hear, its very nature is such as to be heard: one that is so different from the commandment (Law) which also is indeed heard but bestows no righteousness although it is heard endlessly.

Right "out of" the Gospel, which one is made to hear, comes the justifying faith. The faith in Christ kindled is what matters in God's courtroom – to this faith God substitutes His own righteousness to the individual with such faith. Crucial to what men are made to hear is "Christ's utterance" – and this is the whole trouble, "in fact, the rejection." What makes men hear, must be "Christ's utterance" which is the utterance of faith – which was commissioned to the Apostles to preach: this alone makes men hear. Many preachers today lack the quality of being commissioned; what they preach therefore is not Christ's utterance, hence men cannot be made to **hear**.

The prophets, Apostles, Paul, Stephen, etc. were all commissioned and therefore these Jewish men were made to hear the gospel. Yes Christ's own utterance acted as the medium for Isaiah's message as it did for the Apostles. Jesus Himself being the Chief Cornerstone (Ephesians 2:20) of the Gospel Promise with its means of Grace.

These men who were made to hear – that means, Christ's own utterance is what they were made to hear. The fact that Christ came 800 years later does not affect the inner relation of Isaiah's Gospel message. All physical descendants of Abraham and the whole world have heard the Gospel message which was spread as widely for the Jews as what the heavens declare and the firmament shows.

- From the very start and on through the centuries, there was not a single Jew that did not get to hear.

The Old Testament, i.e. Isaiah 53 and what Jesus says about Moses in John 5:39, demonstrates what they heard. He (the Jew) at first heard the prophesy regarding the Messiah and then the fulfilment came and began to spread with rapidity: No one was there who had not heard at least the prophecies. Also Stephen's entire address is pertinent i.e. "... You stiff necked and uncircumcised in heart and ears, you do always resist the Holy Ghost" (Acts 7:51–52).

- Further still, the vast diaspora of the Jews in Paul's time. There were Jews almost everywhere, scattered "into all the earth ... unto the end of the inhabited earth" and their Scriptures, so full of the Gospel message, always went with them.

As V19 states, even in the case of the world today it is not ignorance above that causes the rejection, as though sins of ignorance are less grave than sins committed in full realization. Ignorance on the other hand excuses no soul of man from sin and death.
- The Truth is this: as the Jews heard the Gospel – utterance so they also fully realized its meaning and what its rejection implied. And as it is in our case today; in our case much is mere pitiful ignorance but much also like the Jews.

They the Jews got to realize the universality of the Gospel, but they expected to include the whole world, not by God's righteousness, to be embraced only as a pure gift through faith and by faith alone, but by righteousness attained by means of Law – 9:31. They relied on the Law – the thing which is impossible.

So as today, the Jews had a strong missionary zeal just like the zeal many preachers of the Word today have, but "not according to knowledge." Our ignorance today is exactly the same as that of the Jews – the ignorance lies in building up a righteousness based on some particular portion of Law, or passage in the Scripture referenced to a particular work like tithing, building churches, donations to some groups in poor countries, meetings of different age groups doing different things etc.

The fruit of Christ's utterance as heard and understood is faith from which the divine power that transforms man is derived. In this case the Jews offered only disobedience and contradiction, the more they read the Gospel, the more violently they refused faith in Christ. The Law and the Prophets, these two divisions of the Old Testament bear the same testimony.

Moses was the first great head of the young Jewish nation when it first became a nation: he witnessed all its unbelief at the start and Stephen tells how it treated him, who preached the Promise – the Gospel of the great Messianic prophet (Acts 7:35-41).

It is this rejection of the utterance which divides the world which is now heading fast to its doom. Where Christ's utterance is rejected, it means multiplication of divisions with serious and bitter disagreements and hatred as indeed we see the different powers all preparing for World War III and absolutely nothing else can save except Christ's utterance.

- So the Word applicable to the whole world: "all day long did I spread out my hands to a people disobedient and contradicting. Behold a house left desolate." (Matthew 23:28)

ROMANS CHAPTER 11:1-36
The Saving Purpose

We live in a world of sin. We are born in sin i.e. in ungodliness thus separated from God. And there is no individual power that can unite man to God into an everlasting union. It is this union in which God's plan of salvation is centered. Salvation is the intended goal for every living soul. This union is the manifestation of God's love and Grace to mankind. In His love all are reconciled to God Himself and to fellow man. And this union is the mystery that those who were once enemies to Him are now the Beloved, the Church. In this union, it is God who does everything for man – which only needs to be accepted as pure undeserved favor (Grace). God's work consists of the following:
1) Election by Grace
2) The Reconciliation of the World (the marvel of divine grace)
3) God's mercy – not as one running or working
   All the above emanate from God.

1) Election by Grace

This is the doctrine in Scripture, the means by which sinners become God's people, the Beloved, His sheep. They are the ones He foreknew to the end of time, those who are brought to faith by Grace. These God chose as His own, as "His people" in whom all His plans were to be carried out. The rest had to be turned to Judgment. As it was in the Old Testament, so it is in the present period of the New Testament, by the same means God makes sinners his own.

These – God's people, have never been the physical descendants of Abraham for whom Elijah pleaded with God to punish Israel – the ones who killed the prophets, knelt before Baal, destroyed the very alters of the Lord, thus overthrowing even the true foundation of God – the very worship of Jehovah. At the time of Elijah there were only 7000 God's own people in the northern kingdom. Even in Paul's time, God's people, the true Israel, only a few of them were left, an estimated of about 25,000 in Judah; only the ones who remained in Abraham's faith. Even at the time of Christ, the true Israel, God's people came to consist of only a portion of the physical descendants of the Patriarchs, the rest rejected the election by Grace.

Election by Grace asks for nothing on the sinner's part, it gratuitously bestows God's righteousness in Christ to be accepted by faith (trust) alone.

With Grace everything centers in the Divine favor and whatever it bestows is absolutely unmerited by the recipients, who do not only merit nothing but the opposite of this favor – eternal death. Grace is universal, equal, sufficient to save all – the rest are not saved and the only answer is – they reject this grace and seek to save themselves by their own means. So the rest of the world is under judgment – it starts with self-hardening – as was in the case of Pharaoh. Then God's judgment strikes – these in petrification, and these are the majority who thrive in works, take vows to keep all laws not knowing that they are dealing in works, the very ones God rejects. We see this judgment having struck our present generation (Isaiah 29:10) – the hearts of men have become hardened as a stone.

- The progressive hardening which occurred to the Jews has struck this generation as well. In fact this generation's hardening is much worse than ever before.

"Let their 'table' – meaning earthly prosperity – be turned into a snare and for their welfare a trap" – this is God's answer. This earthly blessing turned into a curse. All the prosperity of the Jews would no longer be a blessing but a curse – the implication is due retribution! What God gives to the wicked physical Israel is for their wickedness, from Him as rightly demanded by their wickedness.

"Let their eyes be darkened not to see." Convinced that God is still blessing them while they have gone into complete obduracy and that God will not forsake them, and they are made to go on, obdurate as they are until the snare suddenly tightens, the net closes, and the trigger springs the death trap, the recompense, due justice destroys them. But even in that judgment God furthers His plans of Grace.

The Jewish hardening was progressive and so was the progressive judgments which in fact reveal the long history of the Jewish nation. The punitive hardening which follows after self-hardening has fully set in among the rest as described. "They that will, shall not" – the Spirit which is one that is wholly unresponsive.

"That they should not see – should not hear" – V9. That is to say that the Scriptures speak of the matter in a number of places and their testimony is briefly summarized.

- This is what happened long ago and is still continuing to this day. For the Jews obdurately did not come to the final end, and this has been due to God's great longsuffering – His patience with the vessels of wrath already fitted for destruction.

The Jews were never wiped out as one would have thought in retribution as God did in the case of Sodom and Gomorrah; and also it was not the case with the destruction of Jerusalem, for 90,000 Jews were carried away into slavery: to this day "their backs bow down over" – loins shake when the back bends down with excessive load. They live among the bitterest of their enemies.

- These Jews never regained existence as a nation. For almost 2000 years they have been scattered among all other nations, but have remained distinct, never absorbed. Endless indignities are heaped upon them. To this day "Jew" is an opprobrious epithet although they use it unknowingly.

The sum of their history is not that the Jews innocently suffered these centuries of woe, it is that they have ever brought these woes upon themselves anew by rejecting God's ordained means. They crucified their own Christ; to this day their hatred of the crucified Messiah stamps them more than anything else as "Jews" for election they would have none of it. All these help us to understand God's workings: the petrifaction of the Jews goes much deeper than what we are normally able to see.

Like that of Pharaoh (Romans 9:17) whose judgment concerned not merely himself but the world and to the vessels of wrath (Romans 9:22–23) that were borne by God's far-reaching plans of mercy. And to the judgment of the Jews in their hardening in Paul's time – V7 was by no means the end of the matter, not for the Jews themselves only but – 1) God used it to produce a blessed effect on the Gentiles and 2) would use this effect to produce another even on the Jews – i.e. save some of them.

- By their fall – was the salvation for the Gentiles and the Jews themselves were made jealous.

- Such is the astounding mercy of God that he makes even the hardening and the fatal fall of the Jews serve His saving purposes. The jealousy that was created by the spread of salvation among the Gentiles resulted into the salvation of the petrified Jews in the blessings. It also increased the ugly hardening and refusal in the majority of the Jews.

We all know that Paul was a "Gentile" Apostle (Acts 9:15) and we would have expected his glorification of his ministry to lie in what God's grace had accomplished among the Gentiles, but no, there is something more.

All the accomplishments among the Gentiles look beyond the Gentiles, to the Jews, to provoke them to jealous so that some may be saved. The more Gentiles Paul converts, the more of this jealousy he creates, much of it of a favorable nature, which results in conversions of the Jews, and these conversions constitute the real crown of Paul's ministry among the Gentiles.

A remarkable view and yet so true! These conversions include all the conversions of Jews in every city he visited. All the remnants according to an election of grace. This election by grace builds the Church of God or God's people, the remnant.

2) The Reconciliation of the World
(The Marvel of Divine Grace)

"Jewish jealousy" became Paul's motive for the recovery of some – i.e. the remnant. The more Paul's converts, the more of this jealousy he creates, much of a favorable nature, which results in the conversion of the Jews.
- And these conversions constitute the real crown of Paul's ministry among the Gentiles. Remnants as such always according to an election of grace.

The Gentile Christians are not to think that because He is a Gentile Apostle, the Jews no longer mean anything to him or them. It's a warning lest we Gentiles exalt ourselves to our own injury. The glory of God's success among the Gentiles must be viewed from the second point of the effect which it has on the Jews, for it saves some. Totally undeserving people are the real crown of Paul's mission, and yet the blessings to the world.

This is what is astounding: God's casting away the hardened Jewish nation becomes a blessing to the world! As a most spiritually favored nation on earth, its casting away scatters all its blessings over the entire world. What we now see – not only Gentile or world riches but also Jewish remnants – or the reconciliation of the world, which means making the whole world completely different which is used both objectively and subjectively. Subjectively – God's placing a man into an entirely different and most blessed relation to himself by means of faith in Christ without any restriction of any kind to be personally reconciled to God by faith in Christ. Such is the divine rejection of the Jewish nation that even its rejection has, in the **mercy** and in the **providence of God** an effect on the world that is so blessed. There has never been such a nation with such an effect.

This reception continues in the same way even after Paul's own labors long cease and others spread "salvation" in the world. Nothing ever happened to the Gentiles that was similar to God's casting them away as being hardened: but this happened to the Jews. It is in contrast to this that the conversions of the Jews in Paul's day were and in our day still are in the fullest sense of the word, "life from the dead." In a way this is also true of conversions of Gentiles but eminently more so of those Jews. Great is the marvel that casting away is the reconciliation of the world, certainly equally great and like life from the dead that any Jew are still received.

This is the nature of God's love and grace. The first dough made out of the new grain, a portion was always separated and baked for the Lord as a heave offering which sanctified the whole lump of dough.

- The portion separated was not in itself holy nor could it make the mass of dough holy; the holiness lay in its being set apart for the Lord and in accepting it, and being part of the mass of dough and of all dough made from the harvested grain, the whole dough thus became sanctified and blessed. This, the Jews practiced and accepted it at the time as true. The means of making them holy was the root – the Promise. Then also if the root is holy, also are the branches borne by that root. The first cake of the dough and the root denote Abraham with whom the Covenant was made for the Patriarchs.

The mass of the dough and the branches denote all the spiritual descendants – with their undeserved blessing all coming

from God the Giver. These two are the illustrations, yes contravening nature but demonstrate that in the whole world of men, nothing exists that is comparable to what God's love and grace have done and still do to men today.
- The illustration had to be invented of acts that never happen among men that never the less picture the astounding acts of God.

The fatness or sap of the good olive tree, of which all its own branches and its grafts partake. This is the marvel of divine grace – in which the Gentile Christians are to note well, is that they together with believing Jews are made blessed partakers of all that God originally gave to Abraham and the great Patriarchs of the Covenant.

The astounding miracle of grace is here pictured by an equally astounding figure: such a wild olive branch grafted in among the good living olive branches and thereby made a joint partaker of the root of the good olive tree, of its fatness, its rich sap. We should note well! It is not something that this wild olive branch furnishes or is to furnish but the fatness which the good root of the good olive (the promise) furnishes this engrafted wild olive branch.

Of course some branches of the good olive tree (the same obdurate Jews) were broken off – but when we consider the Gentile Christians who were originally pagan and now can be found among the believing Jews – we should see that we must not glory over them as if our being placed among them makes the Gentile superior – because "thou bearest not the root, but the root (grace) thee," – just as it bears the native branches.

Gentiles are utterly dependent on the root and not the root in any way upon thee, otherwise you will start saying: native branches were broken off in order that I on my part might be grafted in – thus certainly considering myself superior – but in what way?

The actual reason for the removal of the branches was by their unbelief, were they cut off, and Gentiles by thy faith they stand among the branches which were not broken off.

So the Gentile Christian stands only by his faith and not by merit, or superiority of his. Faith as trust and confidence is only awakened by the grace and the gift of God's righteousness. Pride and high-mindedness were the marks found in minds of unbelieving Jews. To find such pride in oneself is itself a cause to be afraid lest it does one that it helped to do for Jews.

If God spared not the natural branches, neither will he spare thee. If he did not spare the physical descendants of Abraham when they fell into unbelief, he will certainly not spare thee, a Gentile Christian if you too fall into unbelief. The marvel of divine grace which Gentiles are to note well is that the Gentile Christians are together with believing Jews and are both made blessed partakers of all that God originally gave to Abraham and the great Patriarchs of the Covenant.

How our faith views the matter:
When we look at all the spiritual blessings and gifts that enrich us Gentiles, these should fill the Gentile beneficiaries with profoundest gratitude towards God, to keep out all false pride and glorying and false feelings of security and superiority. Faith ever sees that it has nothing but pure unmerited divine benefactions.

We remain in God's beneficence by faith alone. Once faith is wrought in us by Grace and by the Word, then synergism results. This faith holds fast to God's grace with its power and thus also does not let us fall. In the Scripture beneficence and severity ever appear side by side, are never quiescent (inactive) but always energetic and operative, and never without their effects or manifestations. Any Gentile who does not remain in God's beneficence but falls from it will also certainly be cut off as a dead branch is cut off from the good olive tree into which he was grafted.

Moreover, also those Jews, if they remain not in their unbelief, shall be grafted in, God is able to graft them back in. The Jewish mass that has fallen away in unbelief, some will be won from this unbelief by Grace – God is able to graft them back – V23. So great is God's grace, which even after unbelief has set in, grace is still able to overcome such unbelief. This was true regarding the Jews.

Also see what this grace does to the Gentile – it must first cut the Gentile out of his natural wild olive and unnaturally graft him into the good olive tree. The Jews however never grew out as branches of the wild tree, they were only broken off the good tree, and the natural procedure would be to put them back into their own native tree.

This, the Gentile Christian ought to remember about himself, and about any Jews who may become converted. It is a tremendous deed to pry a pagan loose from his paganism and then uniting him with the converts. If God is able to perform two acts in saving a Gentile, how much more will He be able to perform the one act which is required to save the Jews!

The point however is not that it is easier to save a Jew than a pagan, the point is that if God has done a thing that is contrary to nature, He certainly demonstrates that He is also able and can do a thing that we must consider as "in accord to nature."

3) God's Mercy – Not as one Running or Working

The Word is the bringer of mercy – gracious gift and call. There are many misunderstandings of God's Word, today in particular, to "all Israel" on the basis of (1 Kings 21:1) practically means that the whole Jewish nation shall be saved in the millennium. But this ignores Paul's own context, for instance (Romans 9:7) – not the children of the flesh but the children of the promise. In Paul's time, the same situation existed as was in Elijah's time and so in the present time: those who are saved only a part (a remnant – V5) "election did obtain" and the rest were made like stone, petrified.

- This mystery – which is still taking place but never coming to be realized.
- Those (Jews,) if they remain not in unbelief, shall be grafted in again.

The mystery which Paul reveals is that the Jews will not disappear as one might think. Other nations have disappeared; the ten tribes of the Jews themselves have no trace. Not so the two tribes that constituted Judaism in Paul's time. They will endure until the last Gentile is brought into the Kingdom and the Lord returns for the great judgment – they will endure to the very end!

The Jews
According to one norm enemies, according to another norm, beloved, these are the Jacobs, the believing Jews throughout the centuries. According to the Gospel – at first unbelieving and therefore enemies and personally hostile towards this Gospel: All Jews are reared thus in their Judaism, but when

the election wins them, so that they do not remain in their unbelief, and thus become beloved – constitute remnants according to an election of Grace.

These "**beloved**" **Jews** are not only natural but at the same time spiritual sons of the spiritual fathers, sons restore them to their blessed spiritual connection.
- For the Gentiles they had never had a connection with the Patriarchs before, their spiritual connection was established by God's mercy – gracious gift and call.

Explanations of how Jews who are first enemies V20 of the Gospel are yet allowed eventually to become beloved of God. For unregretted are the precious gifts and the calling of the Gospel– calling by which means we are saved.
- This is generally expressed as God's people and in another way, namely from the angle of God's Word as promises.

These still disobedient Jews are in the position we believing Gentiles once occupied, with our disobedience: as their disobedience brought you mercy, the mercy you have is to bring them the same mercy from their disobedience. So God made no mistake, has nothing to regret in regard to the gracious gift and the call He extended to the Patriarchs and the Jews. All is working out according to His wonderful plan.

It is true, the believing Gentiles were once in pagan disobedience and these still disobedient Jews are in the disobedience that is not pagan but Jewish rejection of the Gospel. The term disobedience covers both conditions. Here we get the final statement and the explanation, the unit that ties everything together and thus leaves nothing further to be added.

God has placed all the Jews and Gentiles on the same level in order to save all of them by the same means, namely mercy.

And this is the mercy in Christ Jesus which saves all of them alike by justification through faith alone. God has placed all the Jews and the Gentiles of whom Paul is here speaking on the same level in order to save all of them by the same means, namely mercy; and this is the mercy in Christ Jesus which saves all of them alike by justification through faith alone.

Both were in disobedience and so all were shut up together, all of them were left with nothing whatever but this, their disobedience. The Jew was not a whit better off than the Gentile; all his rights, prerogatives, claims and boasts were gone, he lay in the same prison of disobedience with the Gentiles. This Gentile would not be high-minded (V21) and look down on the Jew as being one that had fallen so terribly, for his pagan disobedience was the same fearful prison called "disobedience."

Only one door permits anyone to leave this prison and it is inscribed: God's mercy. That is why all else was taken from them; in order that He (God) might "mercy them," bestow His mercy on them from their ungodliness (in contrition) and take away their sins (in justification.) The Jews and Gentiles who in equal disobedience are brought to faith and Salvation by God's equal mercy.

In Rome, the Jewish and Gentile Christians were found together in one Church, in the one good olive tree under this blessed mercy. They had come out of the same awful disobedience. Instead of being supercilious toward others, they had only one thing to do: embrace each other and sing thanksgiving to the one mercy that brought them together in God's own wonderful way. And then they would understand what God and his mercy were doing for others like them, yea, would continue to do until the end of time.

We then come to understand the Promise of salvation in the whole Old Testament which stands so gloriously in the

Old Testament with regard to Jacob whom God renamed "Israel" and from whom Israel obtained its name.

"The Deliverer," the God – (Hebrew – the Vindicator who takes Jacob's part) is the Redeemer: Christ Jesus, God Incarnate. He shall take ungodliness away from Jacob, i.e. the different forms of unbelief away from the Jews and Gentiles will be grafted back into their olive trees – which constitute only part of all "Israel" the true Israel.

The heart of the Covenant which God made with Jacob (Israel) is this taking away of sins – which constitutes the forgiveness of sins according to the election – which is justification by faith – the central doctrine of the Epistle to the Romans.

- This is the original Covenant – from one generation to another – regarding the people of God – with the taking away of their sins.

God's people, namely from the angle of God's Word as the promise.

- The Gentiles profited by the mercy that they received through the Jewish disobedience.

What happened to the Jews is exactly the same as what happened to the Gentiles – as we profited by their disobedience, they are now to profit by the mercy we received through their disobedience.

We the Gentile Christians must consider our case; when the Gentiles were disobedient, when we were pagans and how God made the very disobedience of the Jews work out so as to extend His precious Gospel mercy to the Gentiles, even as they have it now – let us all think about this comparison.

So all believers like Paul should ever be filled with the rapturous praise which filled Paul's heart: "Oh the depth of the riches of God's wisdom and knowledge, His unsearchable decision and untraceable ways." For because of Him and through Him and unto Him – are all things that exist; to Him be glory forever, AMEN.

The Jews were so certain that they were God's people because of their works and so are many today – they are deceived. If there were a people of God, it was ever due purely mercy. As God's people ever and always are: the remnant, it was ever marked by election made by grace and not by works – pure mercy.

ROMANS CHAPTER 12:1-21
Living Sacrifice

The great spiritual change that takes place in man's heart is capsulated in this chapter. It starts with faith in Christ's work of salvation. This change begins immediately after faith has been kindled and continues until finally it ends in death. With this faith the newness in life begins. The change is a result of God's portion of faith – the great transformation from ungodliness into a living sacrifice and consists of the following elements:
1) The Portion of Faith – Our qualification and obligation
2) The Doctrine – Our boundary
3) Love – Our intelligence

1) The Portion of Faith – (Our Qualification and Obligation)

The process begins with God's divine sweet words about His own compassion: tender pities which God extends to man to bring him out of the pitiful state of sin and death. These compassions are received by faith alone. Those who accept these gifts are filled up with God's own love when God's righteousness and the transformation in the soul which animates the body begin and this new life becomes visible. This transformation is not as such an outward conformity, such as we ob-

serve every time the fashions of the world change from one generation to another or the change of mode of worship;
- and it is no less than constant inward transformation
- one that is accomplished by renewing of mind – by making the mind conform to God's divine will which is found in the Word which is the righteousness of God.
- This righteousness is a process – using the organ of man's moral knowing and thinking.
- So that it no longer thinks, understands and judges as it once did and it cannot do so because it is in a process of renewal, that which advances steadily.
- The mind totally ceases its old disregard of God's will, its old folly of contenting itself with its own will – the flesh.
- With the new trust in God (faith,) a Christian subjects his own conception **of what is good to that of God's own will** – only in this manner does one become a member of the spiritual body or a living sacrifice as a result of the "portion of faith."

The faith which God gives to every believer places each one in his own station or place with a particular **qualification (gift)** and **obligation (work)** making all believers constitute one harmonious whole. The portion of faith fixes every believer into the right frame of mind – which places each one into the right place within the spiritual body.
- The great effect of the gift to each believer is to think of its possessor (God) first. Thinking of our possessor first enables us to think of ourselves only as highly as we are compelled by the warranted facts; beyond that lies the sin of arrogance, pride, pomposity, superiority etc.
- Below the warranted facts, lies a silly inferiority complex, false humility, a thinking of what is not true. To think of

God first is to be sober minded, to be of a sound mind as to each one whom God gave a gift which neither exaggerates nor depreciates one's own portion. "To be minded so as to be sober minded," to each one God apportioned the portion of faith. Sober and sane thinking that neither exaggerates nor depreciates such gifts as God himself has bestowed.

- God makes His own apportionment (1 Corinthians 12:7–11) in His own wisdom and His love.
- To appreciate properly the portion you have received is to honor God, it is to be of a sober and balanced mind in regard to your own person.

Portion of faith – is personal saving faith which in every believer possesses some gifts or qualifications to be exercised for the glory of God and the good of the Church.

- And this qualification (portion of faith) assigns the obligation (work) to each believer. (Talent can be only a small part of it.)

To visualize the individual gifts belonging to each individual's faith – all Christians are one body which has many different members that have different capabilities, giving rise to different functions each of which is necessary in its place in this life.

An example is the human body with its many members e.g. hands, legs, eyes etc. and each of these is enabled to perform a specific function all of which form one grand unit of a human body; a lovely analogy of the human body and the members of Christ's Church.

So although we are many, we are "one spiritual body" in Christ, not in the sense of an outward organization as the visible Church, but a spiritual organism, the invisible Church, the great "Una Sancta."

We need to understand what the spiritual body implies;
- It is not so much the relation of each believer to Christ which matters, but what this relation to Christ constitutes regarding all of us as one spiritual body and causes us to be in relation to each other namely; "one by one" we are members of each other reciprocally.

Our union with Christ makes us all individually fellow members. As such a member, I belong to all others and all others belong to me. With such gifts as the Lord has blessed me with, I serve not only Christ, but I serve all the others and all others serve me.
- But what must be brought to each one's conscience? For what is the little I contribute to them compared with the vastness of what they all contribute to me?

Everyone has a gift, grace given to him and it makes little difference whether we understand this "grace" so as to include the grace that saved each one, say Paul, and justified him (3:24) or restrict this grace which made him an Apostle and bestowed charismatic gifts to him.
- So when each one looks to the Lord who gives each one of the believers his portion – he is utterly humbled.
- When he (Paul) looked at his fellow Apostles he was ashamed (1 Corinthians 15:8).
- But when his office and work are assailed by others in the Church, he must think of himself as highly as his office and the Lord's gift for what is demanded of him; and with proper vigor he defends the Word. Paul bids all others to do the same with the same sanity and balance in

whatever station the Lord has placed each one among the many members, in accord with what portion the Lord has equipped them with so that they may contribute to these other members.
- No Christian is to exceed the estimate he must place upon himself. Just like the human body, there should be no conflict within the spiritual body. As only one body we are complete as a human body is complete.

Here is the elimination of pride, selfishness, greed, hate, laziness etc., all the things which disturb unity – it is indeed a new thinking that transforms. A new life which is controlled by the saving faith-portion of faith.

2) The Doctrine (Our boundary)

All gifts together form one whole and they picture each one of us in his proper place. This is how the lives of those people who have been justified by faith look (living sacrifices).
- These gifts are the luscious, abundant fruits that make the tree of God's righteousness by faith alone the very tree of life. There is no believer without a gift.
- That is, all and every gift that enables us to live any part of our Christian life – which gives rise to work or function – as indeed a living sacrifice.
- Gifts that enable us to do miraculous deeds are not mentioned here.

Several gifts are mentioned but each one with the boundary i.e. how to exercise that particular gift. The greatest gift that God gave to man so valuable, so edifying, up-building to the Church, is that of teaching.

- The norm or the boundary for any gift is the Word. This cannot be something subjective i.e. a person's own trust, but in its own nature must be something objective, "the faith" (or the doctrine) that was once delivered to the saints – Jude 3 (that is the substance of the Word).
- The exposition or teaching of the Scriptures, was ever guarded against false expositions and this agrees with "the faith" believed, taught and confessed by the Church as it was received from Christ through the Apostles.

Paul could have straight away said according to the Scriptures but at this time the New Testament was not yet written and the Old Testament did not contain the fulfilment that had come with the fuller teaching of Christ.

- As regards the norm, Paul is simply voicing Christ's own command as given in Matthew 28:20 and according to Luke 10:16 whatever disagrees with "the faith" or doctrine is mistaken, erroneous or false i.e. the exposition or teaching of any scripture is to be judged by the Church. In our visible church today, contradictions are passed as intellect or sincerity.
- Today man has totally misconstrued "the Gospel," gone beyond the boundary of Prophecy. Only the norm for the "prophecy" or preaching is laid down, but for the next six gifts in regard to their exercise – **only the sphere** (results) is pointed out. In the next six items, instead of naming the different gifts, (qualifications) which would lead to different capabilities or work, Paul goes straight to naming

their actual results in their different functions, or work, each with its obligations.
- Functions or works which any Christian may exercise as his ability and opportunity which make this possible.

Ministry – Paul equates it to work (office,) in particular reference to his own work as an Apostle: and in this case the connotation (or hint) is that of a service rendered to **benefit** and **help** others, this being the only motive, all compulsion being absent.
- This is a wide field, each one in his station, Paul in his field of "apostleship" – the control is the prophecy – i.e. the doctrine, what he received from Christ, and the task involved resulting from this gift is teaching.
- Tasks such as teaching must lead to admonishing, then imparting in simplicity. Each one's task in any ministry may differ, Paul's one task was teaching and this is the most valuable gift in the Church.
- Teaching results in admonishing (motivational). It includes instruction, making things plain. It starts with beginners and advances its pupils as far as possible, as such are the right teachers. The Scriptures have been greatly subjected to personal enthusiasms as opposed to doctrines and thus destroying the truth. In this manner there can be no advancing of both pupil and teacher as well in the truth. In effect, no admonitions. (Admonition = counsel, warning and wisdom.)
- The right teaching always passes on to admonitions which stirs up to make the instruction effective in our life.
- Admonishing must touch and stimulate the genuine motive that lies in faith and needs to know and apply the right human and Christian psychology, i.e. the major difference between **Law and grace**.

- Its aim cannot be legalistic but the true fruit of justifying faith which grows out of change with spiritual newness of mind, which results in impartation of the truth as opposed to falsehood.

i. Impartation (single mindedness)
The true knowledge and experience of the difference between legality and grace is the only one that leads to spiritual life and this in short is "simplicity" – a reference to the giver's own motivation and aim which must be single not double, not covertly seeking to secure credit, praise, honor, reward for whatever he imparts – and this leads to the quality of a manager or leader.

ii. Manager or pastor or leader: (joyful mercies)
He that manages fits best with the imperative phrase "in diligence" for anyone who is placed at the head of others for the purpose of performing some task, His motto must be in diligence, haste in good sense, **prompt efficiency,** which lead to the object – "mercy."

Mercy – it will be mercy extended, purely aimed to relieve anyone in distress – most importantly.

In the case of **prophecy (mercy)** the result is salvation from sin and death and the gift of new life. Mercy and the deeds of mercy constitute the mark of a true Christian. And such mercy has a quality in cheerfulness, which greets every opportunity for a merciful deed as a great find that makes one jubilant. So we have the three spheres of: 1) motivational teaching 2) single minded imparting 3) joyful mercies leading to Salvation. These gifts with their quality in exercise – these alone build and grace the Church. And finally we come to the exercising of these gifts – the hand that dishes out these gifts which is love.

3) Love – (Our Intelligence)

There is one divine power that should control all work as coming from God's own undeserved favor, God's love. The essential fruit of justifying faith, which is and must be found in every believer is "the love" – a copy of God's Love.

- Love of comprehension according to purpose, purposes to do all it can for its objects. This is pure intelligence of a New Life.
- With this "love" God loved the world, with this love we are to love our enemies as we love ourselves i.e. fellow believers. Much of the love that exists in our Church today is counterfeit (false) love, which hides itself behind the mask of love and of words that are supposed to have the sound of love.

This love is the opposite of "the wicked thing" or Satan. The whole world lies in the power of the wicked one. **To comprehend is to know the good thing which is spiritually beneficial. So as "wicked" has Satan in the back of it, so the good "flows from God."** So also love that comprehends – one which is based on understanding the fallen nature, and God's divine means to save us. Love is the mother of intelligence!

i) With this love we are all equal. So as regards love among all Christians, not as it is interpreted in our version i.e. that of family affection where there are differences e.g. children, parents, grandparents. But with Christian love or brotherly love, all are alike and stand on the same level but where special honor is due to any one Christian, all the rest should try to be the first in according it.

- In this way Paul bestows all possible and all deserving honor to men, for instance, his assistants, he leads other brethren in doing this and is never greedy of honor for himself.
- As regards the honor – that which is due:

ii) All steam behind our action – **Master's will – the true love which directs our service.**
- As regards diligence, at the back of it must be the seething (from boiling) spirit which must move a man to diligence, and the source of such a **spirit** is the Lord.
- And as regards the Lord, a **slave** whose entire work is directed by His Master's Will. As such was Paul himself, a "slave" of Christ. Christ is the Master of all Christians.
- In all their diligence, in all their inner fervor, they heed and obey and do the will of the Master alone. When we act and work as slaves as regards our Master, all the speed we develop in our diligence, and all the steam we generate in our spirit will be directed in the right channel – so that we may benefit our age with our free service because the days are wicked. This is the true love which directs our service.

iii) Always rejoicing in our afflictions when the world hates us (for not shaping to the world.)
- As regards the hope – the glory on the basis of hope, the subjective hope. Joyful hope lifts over present affliction and patient endurance is maintained by steadfastness in prayer. This world hates believers and it is this hate which inflicts us in tribulation through which we enter the Kingdom.
- So we must not try to avoid the affliction by shaping the Christian doctrine, practice, conduct, so as to avoid offending the world. In this manner so many resemble the children of this world.

iv) As regarding the needs of brethren love is the bond of the Church, "Fellowshipping" and contribution (Galatians 2:10), intended to relieve the needs of believers in Palestine. Believers from far and near helped and this was intended to cement the whole Church together. Such fellowshipping helps to cement the Church in a spirit which is considered by all Christians as one family, all of them pilgrims in this world, all of them clinging together as such pilgrims in this world.

The pagans observed that although they (the Christians) have never seen each other, they treat each other as blood brothers. Hospitality is literally to be chased after as one hunts an animal and delights to carry the loot home. V14, the natural man (without love) curses his unjust persecutors, love prays for them that they may repent and that God may pardon them.

v) Love rejoices for having been persecuted for Christ's sake. Let us glory in our tribulations – those that come as a result of our faith in Christ. So rejoicing and weeping are not mere contrasted opposites but go hand in hand.

vi) Harmony, reciprocity.
- The true consensus due to a harmonious mutual relation can only result from **love of understanding**, minding the same thing for each other and it is this which is the source of unity (15:5), but here towards each other which is reciprocity (mutual benefits).

The reason for this unity and reciprocity is simple, we were gifted on the same basis (undeserved favor,) – filling our hearts and minds with the same love of God – understanding and purpose and this draws all believers together, the opposite of setting high things for oneself.

- Love – the true fruit of justification by faith makes men humble – the very opposite of the root of unchristian ambition because he thinks himself extremely sharp, (wise in his own counsel).

vii) All judgment is left to God.
- Nowhere does the Scripture annul the principle of strict justice, a man who does evil ought to be paid back with evil – **but a believer knows the basis of his being** *accepted* – this love of understanding accepts base treatment inflicted and commends his case to God.

This fruit of love springs from a source, a mind that is set toward things which all men, must approve as "excellent" – the Gospel – which must not be injured in the sight of men. So we can see the very source of transformation – love suffers baseness from any man – mind glued to things excellent in all men's eyes (the Gospel) and the result is to be at peace with all men!

This however may not always be possible. The most peaceful Christians may be set upon by snarling, biting dogs and may have to defend Christ, the Gospel truth. So a Christian may appear as a knight that is fully armed and enters battle (Ephesians 6:10). But whilst in the midst of this battle – we should know, as indeed Paul knew – that a just Hand than yours and mine rules and will indeed, in the most perfect justice mete out full due to every rascal.

Love knows no natural justice.

In the first place, love knows that man's natural sense of justice is paralyzed. Imperial Rome was noted for Law and justice, and like all our courts today this can only be said from legislation and only in its moral bearing aspect. But we know that evil and injustices have engulfed almost all legal systems. We should not be alarmed!

A mighty and just Hand is in control – our course of conduct is not to avenge ourselves; by not avenging ourselves we do not abandon right and justice, do not enthrone viciousness and injustice, but turn the whole matter of attending to justice over to God.

- Our own wrongs may well swell out of proportion in our own minds. By exacting justice we ourselves should fall from justice. It is therefore a relief to be rid of this responsibility for which we are incompetent. Even human judges are not allowed to try their own cases.

All such gracious conduct is a result of love – which then Paul makes reference of by calling all those of faith "beloved" those with the same love as that of God. We are to step aside and not to get into the way of wrath with our dealing with justice.

God has long ago settled the whole matter about exacting justice from wrongdoers. Not one of them will escape. Perfect justice will be done in every case and will be done perfectly. But this fruit of love goes very far, it hopeth all things, even conversion of those who appear beyond hope. Therefore if thine enemy comes to hunger, be feeding him, etc. But really the sum of love – do not let evil gain one victory after another over you! But in every battle gain victory over evil with love.

Each one therefore perfectly filled with God's gift of faith (qualification) and obligation work, we all become members of the spiritual body under the control of the one doctrine (the Faith) we are then able to love one another with perfect intelligence as the living sacrifices.

ROMANS CHAPTER 13:1-14
God's Rule over the World – Authority

The divine power which transforms man's heart is God's righteousness through faith as a result of the great work of Christ on the Cross, which washed away our sins and freed us from eternal death with the gift of spiritual life. This spiritual life enables believers to live peacefully under any secular government of the world at large. To begin with, all authority is from God and it is God's own doing that such a thing as government authority and power exists among men.

- God has issued no decree on the subject as to what type of government but has constituted men so that in any community, large or small, they may live in peace and this means it must have some sort of authority to enforce order.
- And from the way God has made man, we see His will for us – to live in peace with fellow man.
- God's authority should spread out to all grades and ranks of such authority, as the government structure under which we must all subject ourselves to.
- No popular authority is specified, whether socialistic, republic, democratic, etc.
- Also whether authority is exercised in a noble form or in an oppressive manner, whether it was attained in a legitimate or in an illegitimate way, neither limits nor qualifies the Christian position – that of submission to that authority. One implication is – anarchy is not according to the will of God for it is abolition of all authority including government authority.

The object of government authority from the point of view of both the governing body and the governed means all rulers everywhere are under God's appointment. The fact that rulers fail in their primary functions is an incident not discussed here. First then, the scripture introduces God's own authority over men:
1) God's Authority
2) God's Love
3) God's Righteousness

1) God's Authority

It should be ingrained – firmly fixed in the believer's mind that no man has authority over fellow man except that which is from God. Every government, any authority that they all have comes from God. In other words they are all accountable to God. Whether the governed know this or not does not change the facts. When Paul wrote, he certainly had in mind the Jewish authority which forced Pilate to send Jesus to the Cross and his own violence as a rabid tool of the Sanhedrin which led to the martyrdom of so many of the first Christians.
- The fact that authority may act criminally changes nothing about God's will regarding their establishment among men.
- The flesh may question that but the Spirit does not.
- The authority from the highest to the lowest administration is God's providence, without which none of them could exist.

- A striking example of the hardest ruler that has ever lived is Pharaoh. God indicates His providential purpose in raising him to the throne.
- Evil (hardened) rulers are often sent to punish a nation even to the point of wrecking its existence.
- The history of the kings of the two Jewish kingdoms (Israel and Judah) is most illuminating and certainly the history of the Sanhedrin and the Jewish kings of Paul's time.
- Yet in the entire domain of God's providence, the ways and purposes of God are unsearchable and untraceable to finite minds. Arranging oneself against the government authority is withstanding the very arrangement of God.
- The rebel or revolutionist may think that he is fighting only men: the Christian is to know better, such men receive a judgment, the very verdict of God.
- But the authorities, to arrange themselves against God such as to muzzle the preaching of the true Messiah was not in any way the arrangement of God. But what then is God's objective of such authority?
- God wants rulers everywhere to be what Paul states: they are that by God's arrangement, administering justice and they condemn themselves when it descends to injustice and also:
- The world is full of wicked men and God has placed rulers among them to check and control this wickedness by means of Law and penalties. All of them being directed not against good deeds but against evil deeds.

Luther states:
- "It is God's way to hold the world which is full of bad fellows in check by means of bad fellows as rulers."
- Laws and penalties deal with citizen's deeds, they deter them from bad deeds and thus keep them glued to the good.

- Good or bad used in a secular sense as men's government regard a deed good or bad, in what is called the justice, in the plain of natural right and justice.

Natural man would even scoff at such laws i.e. God's arrangement. But the fear of their rod, the sword should deter them from doing the wrong. The motive for doing the good for the citizen is the lowest motive of fear. Government works with compulsion, with police force, with military power. It does so in the nature of the case, and must do so, and even God's saints are subject to this secular power. **But the motive for God's saints is that of praise for God's providence, the praise for the law abiding citizen.**

The duties of the authorities;
- God's ministry to thee is the authority in return for the obedience of the citizen. Duties include:
    i) Protecting thee and aiding thee as a member of the community and the state.
    ii) Paul calls them ministers because the exercise of their duties is God's own arrangement.
- Their abuse of office does not affect the main issue.
- The New Testament lays down no law for secular state on any matter. This is left to natural sense of right and justice found among men, who also bear the responsibility for the Laws they put into force and must bear the consequences: whether these are beneficial or detrimental.
- Whether government should inflict death penalties or not is left for the state to decide.
- Christians need to realize God's divine authority in the scripture – in Paul's admonition. Paul wrote this letter towards the end of his work among the Gentile world in

Asia and Europe. Paul was a Roman citizen. Nero having been the Emperor for three years had not yet developed into the monster that he later became.
- The Jews including Paul had experienced hard times under King Herod the Great, the persecutor of Christians.
- They had had the bloody Sanhedrin which crucified Christ, allowed Stephen to be stoned, employed Saul as their agent of bloody tyranny.
- And the Sanhedrin operated under their theocracy when its frightful violation of God's own civil laws occurred.

But all these changed nothing regarding God's arrangement of the state authority.

Like God's institution of marriage stands, no matter what abuses men perpetuate. Like also His institution of Christian congregation and of the Christian Church stands despite what some congregations and some Church bodies do. To imagine for one moment that God is involved in some tyranny and some bad Christian leaders is a misconception. But God reckons (makes judgment) with every one of them.
- No Nero or authority can possibly alter the facts and the principles laid down in the scriptures.

The authority is equally God's ministry in regards to thee, compelling thee to do what is good. Criminals, citizens and believers equally owing the same duty to all God's ministers, subject to the authorities for fear of the rod and also because of the conscience which seconds the wrath that would be inflicted on them.

Subjection to conscience – one being an outer necessity which the citizen cannot escape by outward means of fear of the rod – the lowest motive. The other an inner necessity which holds him even more firmly because of whatever consciousness of God he still possesses. The wrath equals the penalty that would be inflicted for non-subjection, this penalty evidencing God's wrath against us – that of eternal death.

The conscience functions in many non-Christians – at times fails to do so among Christians nor does the fear of punishment always deter.

- The same is true with regard to rulers. It is however true that the Christian is held most strongly by his conscience – at least when properly enlightened. Worldly men often have so little conscience in regard to God's arrangement.

As Christians, we are to act intelligently as well instructed Christians in duly giving to all their dues. Whatever may be due to the representatives of government under which God has placed us, the taxes, the honor that is rightly due from citizens must be given in submission to the government. This must be the believer's way because government is God's ordained means.

2) God's Love

Christians are surrounded by all secular contacts – all other secular people, contacts in communities, in addition to the authority; and one word is needed to regulate his entire secular conduct – God's love He who first loved us. Christians always owe something to the rest and it is this debt or obligation which must not only be permitted to stand but of necessity must be let to stand. This debt is love which is new every morning like the light of another day. And even when stretched to the limit you can never get through it (i.e. cannot completely extinguish the obligation).

All other debts the Christian can and should pay off, but the debt of love never ends. This debt which never ends (which is also mentioned in 9:12) is the love of understanding and corresponding purpose (intelligence). It is like the anticipation of a danger and moving instantly to remove that threat. Like the love of a mother applying her intelligence in detection of danger and removing that threat to save her child Paul states the reality which is startling – it is similar to God's very love to us. By our constant loving, the debt of love is never paid off; and yet by our constant loving it is already paid off! For it is Christ who has fulfilled the Law. Yes indeed the paradox is true.

"Never paid" – always already paid and only then has fulfilled the law.

"Has fulfilled" – meaning has done so in the instant of his loving.

It is so true that "this love" which is intelligence and its purpose is the entire summation of the Law – God's very Word. Love of another human being is the whole of the first and second table of the law (the spiritual body). The essential substance of all commandments and any such as God put into our consciousness **is about our relation to other fellow men – which is expressed in one statement;**

"**Thou wilt love thy neighbor as thyself." (Leviticus 19:18)** The substance of which is the **fear and love of God** also known as the **Gospel**. The fulfillment of this Law is salvation of fellow man.

This is an energy that works, namely with intelligence and purpose. It is not possible to remain inactive. In this respect it is God's love – (John 3:16) – the whole Gospel; God so loved the world (i.e. when ungodliness filled the earth) that He gave His Son, that whosoever believeth, shall have everlasting life – desireth of salvation of another or neighbor and all humanity. This is the true love.

Thus it does not work ill, it only works "good." As to the meaning of neighbor, the one with whom our love comes into contact (Luke 10:29), the man from Jerusalem to Jericho. It desireth and worketh salvation through the Gospel.

This calls forth for a lot of energy, for its fullness is its fulfilment of the Law. **The activity that comes out of our true knowledge of God's Word** (the spiritual body or invisible Church). Therefore, this love is the light shining in darkness – and this love is unity among believers.

3) God's Righteousness
(This love is the light shining in the darkness!)

With this love believers realize that we live in the nick of time, a period with certainty as distinguished from other periods before Christ's first coming. It is a time in which we all must be aroused from sleep, from slumber because our salvation is nearer to us now than when we first came to believe, our very transfer into heaven – is very near. It is night time, the daybreak is near. This night is the present world age and the day is the heavenly age to come. This night ends with the beginning of the everlasting day of blessedness and glory "the Parousia." Even when we first came to faith, the breaking of the day has come nearer to us.

The night of this world with its black pall ever deepening into sin and more sin, had certainly lasted a long time since Paul lived thousands of years ago. Now over 2000 additional years have passed. This night has now certainly cut forward still closer to the sudden break of the final day. Christ warned us that His return would be like a thief coming in the night, suddenly and unexpectedly in the very hour when many are sure that He will not come.

We can do only one thing: be ready every moment, be aroused while so many sleep:

(2 Peter 3:4–14). Let us put away, therefore, from ourselves the works of darkness and let us draw on the weapons of light. The night with its works of darkness – the sin power 5:12 with its "death" which leaves no one out because of the ungodliness.

- With its works of darkness which matches the night, as long as this world age lasts and so the night continues (the ungodliness continues).

"The works of darkness" go on continually and we Christians live in this world age and constantly beset to join in these works. Paul's admonitions let us (Christians) once and for all separate ourselves from all such works so that no solicitation to join in them and no inward desire to join them may contaminate us.

- As heavily armed soldiers constitute his panoply for standing in battle, (Ephesians 6:13) etc. so the Word is our greatest weapon to guard the inside and the outside of the body in this time of darkness. What protects a Christian is the Truth – God's Word or the Gospel with its weapon of **RIGHTEOUSNESS** which we have received through faith in Christ.

This gracious gift of righteousness received as a result of our faith in Christ is our full equipment which we must put on. And this weapon of righteousness is the light that distinguishes us from darkness (Ephesians 6:13), the panoply of God (the equipment of light) which refers to God whose great attribute is light, who is ever victorious over the devil or the darkness.

Paul wants himself and all of us Christians to be clothed in full panoply of the light, during this night of this dark world age, in which the devil rules to a great extent and continues until the day arrives. The moment that day arrives, all fighting will be over.

So we are to fight the good fight of faith here during the night; our weapon of the light is to drive "the works of darkness from us." We are not merely to stand in shining armor to do battle, to stand victorious until the Lord arrives or calls us away before He arrives.

Let us once and for all clothe ourselves, that is – walking continuously and extensively as in the day time when everybody sees and not as in the night time when no one sees. Unbridled acts or other kinds such as strife and jealousy of which the world is full and much of which is found in Church as well. These are only samples of works of darkness of which our conduct must ever be rid. Not only must the fully developed growth be absent but equally the little poisonous sprouts that the devil's seed tries to start everywhere. Exactly how do we completely put off the works of darkness? It is done as Paul tells us: "Put on the Lord Jesus Christ". This is the one heap of all weapons of light; this is done by using two major spiritual weapons.

Christ is put on in two ways:

First as the garment of righteousness, the instant our faith appropriates Christ's death and His merit i.e. the Resurrection (Isaiah 6:10, Matthew 22:12 – the wedding garment).

Secondly as our armor of defense and offense (Ephesians 6:13) which is the act of faith when it uses Christ as the power of sanctification. He is the embodiment of weapon and our full panoply – the spiritual body with the word of truth – the very light shining to the world – the unity of the Church – the minding of one another as a result of God's love.

Forethought cannot match the power of sin in our bodies, not even asceticism which is actually foreign to the Scripture. All derogation of the body as something despised cannot help, as though the sooner we rid ourselves of it, the better.

In this life the body, the soul, the inner man, is so responsive to sin – 6:12 and so are the bodily members – 7:23, such that even clothing, food and drink, a house and a home may stir up lusts, the bodily senses so easily inflame lusts, herein lies the danger. When the day comes and ushers in Christ's Parousia, our vile bodies will be made like His glorious body, and all contaminations by way of the body will be forever removed. Amen!

ROMANS CHAPTER 14:1-23 The Intelligence – (True Knowledge that attains purpose is – the Harmony in the Church)

The knowledge that attains purpose is referred to as the light shining in darkness. This light is very noticeable in worldly technological developments in almost all fields: buildings, medical, aviation, communications, etc. Sadly the end result is not so noticeable with regard to God's knowledge. The One Church of God spoken of in the Scripture, with all members in harmony and unity with peace, joy and a new hope is scarcely noticeable anywhere, and this would have been the real light shining in darkness. This Chapter reveals our erroneous teaching which fails in its admonition on the part of the teachers, resulting into failure to comprehend on the part of the pupils, failure to make a distinction between Law and Grace, which should be the purpose resulting into unity. A most regrettable state of affairs of the Church! The results of errors are the hearts of many that are filled up with our own subjective worldly ideas as opposed to the objective faith; the faith or Christ Himself. Knowledge that attains purpose i.e. unity which would be visible to all human kind which would in turn be the light shining in darkness – the intelligence consisting of the following:
1) Admonition
2) Comprehension
3) Purpose

1) Admonition

Acquiring knowledge of the Word which does not lead to enlightenment of the heart fails in its admonition. Among the Christians, such teaching leads to the divisions of the members between the weak and the strong instead of brethren living in peace, joy and new hope. In such a case the weak passes judgment on the super intelligent brother, thus the weak making himself a master in another person's house, while the super intelligent rubbishes the weak brother, taking him as nothing or a fool, the same person for whom Christ has paid the same price. Failure to understand the Christian doctrine is termed as weakness, while some rubbish the weak and the super intelligent ones, tend to rely on their strength – and they who rely on their strength, with it they fall.
- Both are serious weaknesses which must be removed from the Church.

Many "strong" brethren usually want to take immediate action or measures with zeal to remove those weaknesses by disputation of opinion (arguments against the wrong) but to remove such weakness, by demanding an immediate change cannot be the solution; and in most cases such an approach instead of gaining its laudable end, only defeats itself.

The degree of comprehension by **the measure of qualifications** in God's Word, producing the super strong intelligent experts does not work so well in matters of God as it does in secular education. Even in secular matters, there are very many casualties where purpose is not attained. The problem of lack of true knowledge of God's Word is a delicate one. It would be quite simple if it were a case of true and false, right or wrong. It is not such a case and must not be treated as such.

To do so would be worse than ignorance on the part of the educated, qualified and experienced person, and as such has led to the divisions with the many different forms of worship, segregation, eating and not eating, different days of worship, etc.
- On the other hand, lack of true knowledge leads to serious weaknesses, narrowness, limitations and judgmental attitude.
- The common results of both strong and weak, is that man tends to see other men's faults and constantly wants to doctor them and this makes up much of our preaching today; where we ourselves make good patients.

That the fault of the weak would be as bad as the fault of the strong – and the sin is that of being against brotherly love i.e. lack of intelligence. Both weak and strong would become worse and when one seeks to harm the other, disruption of harmony would be the result.

The disruption:
- The weak sets himself up as if he were the real master in the Lord's house; and separates himself, taking away a few others.
- The strong can only be strong through the Lord's Grace, but to trust in one's own strength is the most dangerous weakness. All the strong should remain so as standing by the Lord's strength, but by themselves with their educated class together they fall.

Food and days of worship are given as examples, as only a few among the long list of non-essentials used to blaspheme or abuse the Gospel. All such non-essentials which can be misused to divide the congregation are referred to as adiaphora.

- In the Gospel liberty one may eat all foods and prizes all of it equally highly while another eats one kind of food and prizes all of it higher than all other kinds.
- This is also true with regard to days, one judges one day better than another while another prizes all days.

It is the weakness of the one who regards some food or some days beneath other foods and other days, but he who judges every day the same must do so, by his own conviction in his own mind without casting a reflection on the other.
- In this manner some Christians chose the Sabbath or Sunday as the day of worship.
- Knowing that it was their privilege to do so, following the right motive in mind and conviction – and to the Lord he minds it.
- Such a man thinks only of the Lord and casts no reflection on others because he knows that they too are most earnestly devoted to the Lord.
- In this spirit of liberty we still observe Sunday, not as being commanded but as serving our need for regular public worship.
- Legalistic ideas are still projected into Sundays, a spirit that is totally foreign to Christ, to the Apostles and the Christian Church.

The right mind and motive should be to enlighten with the Word which alone can lead to enlightenment or intelligence and that is Harmony.

Our entire personal relation is this that none of us who is a true Christian i.e. enlightened – lives or dies except as "another's household servant" – meaning;

- Our service is not for ourselves as though we were our own masters. Our love, desire, honor are directed towards another brother (spiritual body).
- We have given up living according to our foolish blind notions and foolish desires – we live as God's own – and we know what this means – even in death we turn our souls to Christ, commend ourselves to Him and die in the faith; that is being faithful unto death. This is the full sunlight of the Gospel truth – our portion of faith: as members of the spiritual body.

So we cannot make an exception in matters of non-essentials such as food and days of worship. This indeed would be the height of folly. Accordingly when living or dying we wholly belong to the Lord and to be His is our joy and blessedness, our purpose and intent.

- Thus to be His, to belong to Him, is the great fact that motivates us in this life and in death. This translates into God's love for one another.
- And it is for this reason that Christ died and became alive – and was made thereby "both Lord and Christ" so that we too may be His own and live under Him in His kingdom, and serve Him in everlasting righteousness, innocence and blessedness.

Our living or dying to the Lord is a reference to our **living under grace**, and thus establishing him in our hearts as the judge both now and at the final judgment. So the strong and the weak should stop their judgmental attitudes in matters of adiaphora. If we have been guilty, now is the time to repent and amend – remove all the flaws of our ignorance and conduct. Apply our full intelligence in what Christ has gifted us with.

And on the last day, when all men shall acknowledge God as God, shall give an account for setting his weak brother at naught – "worthless fool" – or having judged his strong brother in a matter of non-essentials. Those adiaphoric matters are in themselves innocent and harmless and remain so when in Christian love for each other, we let them alone, but become serious when we as strong or as weak brethren forget to love each other.

Not only in matters of adiaphora are we not to judge each other, but ever to abide by the judgments which God will pronounce. Our resolve must stand: never to hurt our brother spiritually nor much worse to kill him spiritually.

The questions about food and other adiaphora are not a matter of faith but a matter of knowledge. Men's reasoning, persuasions, convictions, have had disastrous effects on fellow men because many times such views of men are based on narrow, weak ignorance or unenlightened consciences. No such subjective reckonings can make anything objectively unclean; no subjective opinions ever in the least altered an objective fact. These are matters already settled by the Lord Himself. The only way open for all believers – is Paul's own admonition "Be strong in the Faith" or be strong in the Word – reference to the true knowledge that makes a distinction between Law and the Gospel – the true enlightenment.

2) Comprehension

To be strong in the faith is certainty or a firm condition needed. The true knowledge according to which **genuine love always acts** and thus also attains its intelligent purpose.
- The love that knows what the Lord's Word really says and what it requires for making the weak strong and the strong confirmed.
- Such love never uses food or disputations about food to hurt anybody's feelings – its own intelligence and purpose forbids such self-defeating folly.
- It may take time to free a weak brother from his unnecessary scruples, in fact the strong would not make a mistake of making a brother nothing or a fool, because of such a thing as food or anything that may cause grief or pain to a brother.
- Love instructs with all kindness, it forbears with all gentleness. It advances a pupil as far as possible.
- But when the weak brother starts to judge, to set himself on the judgment seat, then it is no longer a question of food, but presumptuous arrogance.
- Then love will enlighten Vs 1–2, i.e. it will teach or correct and admonish, and will even grieve (2 Corinthians 7:9).

Strong in the faith – will not let their good be blasphemed. This good is the Kingdom of God. Blaspheming would be like cursing the Kingdom of God.
- The Christians to be divided because of such things as eating, clothing, cutting off hair, etc. makes outsiders make sport of believers.
- Unfortunately the Christians have furnished the occasion with the reasons for the kingdom to be blasphemed.

What we must always remember is that the Kingdom of God is **the rule of God's** grace.
- So all earthly concepts of Kingdoms do not determine this divine concept of God's kingdom or rule of grace.
- This Kingdom does not consist of activities on our part such as eating, drinking and the like.
- Outside observances have too often been made part of the kingdom, though sedulously practiced; they are always not spiritual in qualities and not at all part of the Kingdom.
- They were practiced by the weak in the faith, acted as though they were strong, yes, as if they would do some of the ruling in the Kingdom.

The rule of Grace in the Kingdom of God is evidenced by the **three states** – in fact our very assurance.
- The first and fundamental essential state is "**righteousness**" when God declares us righteous with its result of **peace**.
- And with both righteousness and peace there goes **joy** as a result of sanctification, the joy that glories on the basis of **hope** even amidst tribulations.

The three states of peace, joy and hope reveal our living connection with Christ when the Holy Spirit enters our hearts by faith and Baptism. The three states of righteousness, with its peace, joy, and hope are wrought (worked) by Grace – and where Grace works, these are found. God's Kingdom is also to be found. Before this state we were prisoners, but now acquitted and at peace with God and happy in that peace– and this is our assurance that we are in this Kingdom.

This Kingdom is God's relation to the Christian and thus our relation to Him which is established by Grace.

This Kingdom is not to be taken as a relation of men to men – the modern view today is sadly widespread, which includes all those who "work" for the spreading of the Gospel by establishing a better social, economic, governmental environment, personal justice in the world, by reforms, abolition of wars and all types of uplifting movements.
- Men may mend and patch – God knows the world needs it and the devil ever keeps tearing new holes to be mended. God knows it all and lets it be.
- But all this tinkering and even its best results are not the Kingdom of God, for His Kingdom is spiritual, eternal and not of this world.
- The right relation to God automatically produces the right conduct. Placed in a new relation and fitted with the power of Grace that placed us there: the result is visible.
- "Keep serving Christ" (a reference to all saints).

Presenting our members as slaves to God, freed from the dominion of sin – not having a will of our own but being directly controlled only by Christ's will. Not to set at naught a weak slave, not to judge a fellow slave who is stronger than we are, all our orders being from our Master who bought us with His bloody death, not to obey our flesh. Such a slave to Christ, submits his entire will to Him and all he does, is well pleasing to God and need never fear (this is the assurance – peace, joy and hope) to stand before God's judgment seat.

The conduct: we make **our will be that of our Master Christ** – His will is our own, and His essential virtue grows out of our new relation to God in the Kingdom. Well pleasing to God, that means – the only test believers stand is namely; that they let Him and His Grace *rule their wills* in this kingdom. As tested out for men: Christ presents the slaves so test-

ed to men as being valuable to men, not the character men approve. In fact the more the world hates that slave – a true slave of Christ furnishes no just cause to men to blaspheme the Gospel, and he would if he followed His flesh by acting contrary to His Lord's will in such matters of adiaphorous.
- And as such, a will is the assurance that leads to confidence.

3) Purpose (distinction between law and grace)

The result of our assurance is confidence – the pursuance of the things such as belonging to peace, whereby we edify one another: that instructor improves intellectually one another – which is the spiritual strengthening of all that pertains to our faith and our inner life.
- The things of up-building for each other, things that belong to our mutual up-building which are based upon the foundation of the "Apostles and the Prophets" – which are Jesus Christ Himself being the Chief cornerstone – mutual up-building.

What our confidence must depend upon is "the faith" – a reference to our subjective faith but as including the objective faith of Christian truth.
- In particular also that part of it which produces liberty in all adiaphora for the believer. Confidence is made up of; the faith which results into subjective faith which is the degree of **enlightenment**, **assurance** and **confidence** (or in one word – intelligence) regarding the Christian liberty.

- Being strong in the faith, this person must not suppose that he already has all the enlightenment, assurance and all the safe confidence.
- To be sure of the faith you have, be directing it towards thyself, to clear thyself of wrong to thy brother and not toward thy weak brother and the mistaken scruples he still has.
- This is the trouble with us believers: we see the other man's faults and constantly want to doctor him, whereas we ourselves, we still make a good patient. Our faith in "the things of peace," leads us to move safely in our liberty.
- Our liberty does not consist in this, that each of us is free to do just as one pleases.
- Not being entirely free to do or not to do, to use or not to use, each of course makes a choice but in doing so looks to his brethren.
- To what will benefit those most in promoting peace and harmony and especially in aiding to build up each other – in the faith.

Liberty.
Liberty is precious but it carries with it responsibilities. Like all good and precious things, it must be used with good sense and purpose – the Scripture says: "Be not destroying the person" – be not tearing down the work, a reference to the strong who might be inclined to use liberty unscrupulously to mock the over-scrupulous and the weak.
- The motive is that Christ died for that person: "God's very work."
- Any use of Christian liberty which disregards the damaging effect it may produce upon a weak brother is a bad use.
- To cause stumbling is not the way to being strong, for the weak might be destroyed in his weakness.

- Nor is it intended to confirm the weakness by making it the rule for all the strong – it is again not the way to this end.

Love – the way of Liberty

The way of liberty is love (intelligence and purpose) that it yields so as to enlighten, strengthen and thus to lift above weakness. When I abstain, the weak brother must know that I do so only because I am prompted by love, only for his sake, only because his weakness is weakness and not strength, only because I would give him time and help him to grow strong.

Judgments

The faith that bars out judgments: blessed is the man who does not think of acting as his own judge but let's God judge him, ever submits to his faith, his convictions and his actions to the judgments laid down by God in His Word.
- The Pharisees justified themselves, acted as judges in their own case and of course acquitted themselves.
- The strong are too prone to this weakness because they are strong in some degree, bad weakness to despise a weak brother: not in anything must a strong brother trust his own judgment, much worse to make your judgment that of God.

The weak

Then the weak brother, perhaps in order to escape the jibes of the strong, eats despite his "weakness," he thus stumbles i.e. after the strong placing a stumbling block for the weak, which may even turn out to be a spiritual death trap.
- His judgment is between, undecided.
- He lacks knowledge and conviction as to what God's judgment is. His own poor judgment is that it is a no; but what he sees others do urges and crowds him into a yes.

- So he eats and certainly does so "not from faith," from a confidence that is divinely grounded.

This is his sin, pitiful indeed but sin nevertheless, which God must also judge as sin. The greater guilt lies on the strong brother who is guilty of making his weaker brother stumble.
- The extent of the damage to the weaker is also considerable.

It is not safe to do anything against conscience. Everything that is not from faith is sin: in other words, "Whether, therefore, you eat or drink or whatever you do, do all to the glory of God." (1 Corinthians 10:32) What is not done from faith cannot be anything but sin although it may be eating or drinking!
- Faith here now we see – the sure conviction that an act accords with God's will and His Word. A Christian must have that knowledge (wisdom) and that conviction (assurance) and that confidence.
- The very consciousness of uncertainty makes the commission of the act grave. And that applies to "everything" to all adiaphora and also all else, to whatever God has commanded or forbidden.

Not only outright disregard to His will or bold contradictions are sin, but also uncertainty in our actions, misgivings (doubts,) fears that our actions may be contrary to His will – The first sin began with doubt. In the Christian's whole life, only what comes forth as a true fruit of Christian faith is acceptable to God – all else is sin; and vice versa – every sin of ours does not come out of our faith but comes from out of our flesh – so is Augustine's dictum "that the virtues of the heathen are sin" stands; also is the teaching that all works that are done before justification are sin.

So faith really is more than Christian conscience, it is the enlightened Christian's conscience with which faith operates. Personal faith embraces "the faith" (objective,) it justifies and saves at the same time makes alive and dies to the Lord as the Lord. A slave is he whose will is the Lord's. In all departments of life, what comes out of this faith is the true fruit, which the Father glorifies – all else is sin. And this faith (both subjective and objective faith) among believers is the very light that should be shining in the World (the darkness). So man's perfect intelligence is both the outcome of subjective and objective faith – the true enlightenment from the power of the Holy Spirit.

ROMANS CHAPTER 15:1-33
The Holy Spirit (Power)

We now reach the climax of the greatest Epistle that has ever been written, giving us the answers to the greatest puzzles of our lives:
- Why are we born?
- Why are we here and living?
- Where are we going?

In essence what is the meaning of our life? The Epistle to the Romans is heavy in content and thought: it reveals Paul's heart throbbing with praise, praise and even more praise for all Gentiles. Here Paul opens his heart to us, to see, hear and feel its pulse – the heartbeat filled with spiritual life. What moves Paul's whole life is the spiritual power which is;
- Liberty to the captives.
- Sight to the blind.
- The lame walk – (Matthew 11:5).

Yet this spiritual power searches the soul in order to reveal its sinfulness so as to bring it to obedience and thereafter fills it up with God's own Spirit. The One who is in control of all affairs of the world. So Paul reaches the peak of his spiritual life meaning our hearts must also be filled with the same peace and joy and above all with the Hope which is **the peak of spiritual life.** Sadly this condition of joy, peace and hope is definitely not found in many people's hearts. Instead they are filled with temporal earthly joys and strife. And because they do not have the spiritual power, they lack;

- The ability to carry the burdens of the weak (lacking in wisdom).
- The oneness in thought and mind (lacking firmness).
- The joy and peace which would be abounding in the one hope of the resurrection (the fellowship) or sanctification (lacking in confidence).

These qualities the world cannot give but are the result of a permanent gift of God's grace which comes to us through the Scriptures i.e. normated by Christ (the norm) in His Office and person through the obedience of faith. From the first moments of our obedience to the last fight of good faith – is the whole purpose of our existence, and this period be it long or short is the whole period of sanctification – the only period of spiritual vitality whose activities are made up of the following:

1) Sanctification – (the ability of believers which is unity).
2) Wisdom – (the ability to put each other in mind – the competency).
3) Love – (the intelligence, the childbirth of God's wisdom, the Christian bond – apostleship in case of the Prophets, Apostles and in the case of all believers; the Fellowship).

1) Sanctification (the unity – the believer's ability)

Sanctification is this oneness in thought and mind. This oneness in apprehending (understanding) is an ability which is so vigorously enforced in all our earthly skills and professions.

But alas, (to our grief) so lacking in Christian understanding which is always mistaken for enthusiasm, determinism, humbleness etc. and little to do with apprehension if any. We must all be holding one thing in our hearts. With one apprehension of mind, all our differences would disappear – this is the Christian ability which makes both the **weak** and the **strong** – one and the same. This ability was Christ's main concern in His High Priestly prayer.
- "The oneness in the Word."

"Sanctify them in the Truth, Thy Word is Truth" (John 17:17–21) "so that they may be one, as Thou art in me and I in Thee, that they may be one in Him." All of us must be fully clear on what the Word teaches:
- As instructions are fully obeyed in all other fields of knowledge, so should it be in the Oneness in the Word. Having the same mind is the ability that leads to unity with one another.

The **Scriptures** are the one source from which our minds are to draw **"the same thing"** in accord with this **norm** – our permanent gift from God (Christ). This is not merely to be minding the same thing, i.e. all holding the same convictions and thoughts on every important matter, for many convictions might be wrong despite the unanimity with which they are held. Nor is it possible for each man to have his own "views" about the interpretation of the Scriptures.
- It is not correct to say we may agree to disagree (the motto for the visible church today).
- Where oneness of mind and mouth is lost, somebody is wrong, somebody is not glorifying God but himself, injuring the Church, breaking up the unity in the Word in short

misreading of Scripture. This is the very reason why we have divisions, breakups, and this disintegration will become worse in the future.

The Oneness is to be established by "Christ Jesus Our Lord," that is; **His Office**, and **Person** combined.

Christ's office and person!
- What He was in His Office and Person, is His Word: He is made unto us **Wisdom** (Knowledge), **Righteousness** (Peace) and **Sanctification** (Joy). The Oneness in apprehending the instruction of the Scriptures is this oneness which results into one mouth i.e. united in confession.

Confession – this does not mean that all join in the same Psalms, Hymns, Creed, public worship, etc. but that every member everywhere always confesses the one same Gospel truth i.e. Righteousness and Sanctification: whatever part of it may be broached (discussed) – resulting into unity, thereby glorifying God before men. Glorifying means to speak and act so that His glory (the sum of His attributes) may be our praise and honor among men. The Word that tells of Him is one, and our apprehending and our voicing of that Word must also be one, resulting into one conviction and one confession – source and substance being one so it cannot be more than one view or personal view; we cannot agree to differ and say that creedless is the idea as it is today. **This truth must be the ability of believers.**

Now we see what the Scriptures are about:
- From narrow issues and questions regarding meat, it reaches deeper and reaches out to all who are able and unable.
- Our norm is to please God as Christ is our norm. (Righteousness to Sanctification and then joy, peace and hope.)

- Then reach even further to the *unity in the Word and the unanimity* (one mind) with which all should glorify God. And it is thus, we at last reach the differences which divide us. Yet they are aphoristic – things outside the Law.
- Such as Jews and Gentiles – differences which are really like eating and not eating.
- Look at all such things that divide us in the Light of God, the Father of Our Lord Jesus Christ.
- The God with whom our whole salvation in Christ is bound up.
- We have one standard – Christ – Our Lord.

Therefore, be receiving each other in full mutuality, character, and activity since we are all Christ's by virtue of having been received by Him, for God's glory – "the oneness which centers in Christ."

Glorify God with one mind and one mouth strikes two chords (basis of harmony) – Truth and Mercy. All under the banner of the Lord Jesus Christ, ruler of our hearts, united to glorify God with one standard (ensign) or goal **the Hope of our salvation –** the Crown of all our blessings in Christ.

2) Wisdom – (the ability to put each other in mind the competency)

The world was to look at this oneness and would have been attracted to God. The oneness in Christ would have attracted all men of the world – and this oneness would be made up of joy, peace and hope which were manifested in the congregation in Rome. For those who are knowledgeable they look to their "hope." The channel which the Spirit uses is the Word. What fills the hearts of believers – Paul emphasizes here; joy, peace and hope in believing Christ – the great work of Grace. This Hope is the crowning believers' competence (adequately knowledgeable) that Paul was *ever concerned* with, for the rest of his life – even as it was for the Roman congregation. This congregation was really competent – they were filled with all knowledge, the right quality of heart, i.e. the full measure of knowledge to be able to put each other in mind of what is necessary for their faith and life.

- Here Paul truly equates knowledge to being able to put each other in mind.
- A true and perfect judgment because there was no strife, errors or divisions in the Church in Rome, all were aiming for this One Hope of glory. Paul then makes a startling conclusion about this congregation in Rome:

"Now I am convinced, brethren, that you on your part are full of goodness."

- **the necessary knowledge to proceed safely and securely.**
- yet this congregation had never had an Apostle in their midst,
- All having come from different areas and backgrounds.

Yet they had preserved the Word without loss of the teaching they had received, had kept it and they were without strife, error or division.

- They all were filled with one goodness.
- Paul knew of no evils existing in their midst.
- A fine congregation indeed it was.

This letter is indeed written in a bold manner. Paul tell us that he cannot take any personal credit for the special **ability** and competency of the way in which he **has put these things** the Romans have long known.
- "It is not my superior intellect or my dialectical skills, it is wholly the result of Grace given me from God."
- Grace that I have never deserved, that God in His goodness made as a gift to me when He equipped me to be an Apostle.
- That is, whatever they read in this letter – it is not Paul speaking, but the voice of God's own Grace which uses Paul only as its humble, unworthy instrument.
- Paul had become the actual result – the Public Servant of Christ Jesus: i.e. a called Apostle.

Whatever office a believer may hold – it is due to God's Grace and its gift of accomplishing anything.
- In other words, whatever God had bestowed on Paul – was for others. A public servant serves the public (a reference to the spiritual body).
- The letter was part of public service and as a public servant, he writes.
- "It was to be a service pertaining to his whole future work among the Gentiles and so was the letter linked to this public work."

The **quality of his public service** – engaged in serving in a priestly manner.

"The work related to the Gospel"– in order to bring about the offering of the Gentiles as acceptable to God – that which God can fully accept as a true, pure, holy offering. To bring this to pass was Paul's office and work. Paul's one concern was an offering having been sanctified in connection with

the Holy Spirit – set apart and separated from the world – i.e. Wisdom (believing, peaceful, joyful and filled with Hope) in connection with the Gospel – so that we too may ever be in union, in living connection with Christ. Which is also our sanctification – back to where we left off in the last section. Paul has glory – "that I may indeed glory as I do":
- In regard to the things pertaining to God.
- The offering of the Gentiles or the Churches he planted.
- Producing the obedience of faith on the part of the Gentiles by Word and work in connection with power of signs and wonders. The chief means used by Christ, the one which is ever operative in producing the obedience of faith; in connection with the Holy Spirit's power, or in connection with *God's Spirit* – The Word.
- Which means the Three Persons: God, Christ and Spirit.

Christ wrought the signs and wonders, Christ used the Spirit's power or the Power of Grace (the power of the Gospel) the one that is able to produce the obedience of faith. From Jerusalem all the way to Illyricum – amazing at Paul's accomplishments given the time. He lived up to the purpose of the Apostleship which was to lay the foundation where no Church existed. There was also another related purpose for this letter to Rome and his intended visit to Spain; to share in the one fellowship of fellow believers in Rome.

Now at last, the very tide of his work can take him through Italy, truly an amazing spiritual strength – and his longing dates back for many years. The Romans congregation through this letter is to learn about Paul's whole life as it is bound up not only with the brethrens' fellowship; but much more in regard to the overriding purpose of the Gospel – as an apostle of Christ.

- Laying new foundations will drive him to new regions.
- It means the Romans will take full interest in his journey to Spain, help him on his way and send men along to escort him and pray for his success. In doing this they would be exercising another of their spiritual gifts which is Love – to which we now turn.

3) Love – (The Intelligence – the childbirth of God's Wisdom, the Christian bond which is apostleship in case of Prophets, Apostles and for all Believers' Fellowship)

Love of understanding and purpose works "intelligence." We are not to wonder at the amazing fervent vigor or drive back of Paul's missionary work; we are to understand the power behind all his public service. The Romans with the same fullness of grace would understand why Paul took so long to visit Rome. Before Paul could proceed directly to Rome (now in Corinth,) one more task had to be done – to render another public service. Paul still had to deliver the collection from the Asian Gentile congregation, sent to the Jewish Church in Jerusalem that was going through a difficult time and many of its members were poor and needed help. In this public service all the Gentile Churches were drawn together in close fellowship by this act. The power behind this act was the gift of Grace which must be found among all believers – love, the overriding purpose of the Gospel.

a) While the motive of this collection was pure Christian charity, there was also another motive i.e. the mother church of all. And all these – her daughters in the far off Gentile lands were for the greater part made up of Gentile lands, were to be drawn intimately together in close fellowship. By this act of Charity, unity was to be strengthened. Thus the noblest feature of this gift was the exercise of spiritual fellowship; love or the believer's intelligence.
- "Debtors were they to all brethren including the Jews." Who in this case were the ones who delivered the Gospel to the Gentile Churches. All Gentile believers are under obligation (debt of love) to the Jews. If the Gentiles fellowshipped in the Jewish Spiritual things, they are indebted to render public service to them in natural things. The one fellowship deserves the other – the one debt and obligation entails the other. The things that feed the body are only a small return for things that nourish the Spirit.

On the whole, the whole world is indebted to the Jewish believers for the Gospel. In Africa we look at the many white missionaries who ventured into the unknown territories for the Gospel and sacrificed their lives to carry out translations so we could have the Gospel in our languages, yet Africa for whom such sacrifice was made is a sad story as far as embracing the truth is concerned. The effects of the gift of grace are not visible nor are we diligent in the study of God's Word thus lacking in Christian wisdom, ability and competency. And so we have not been as fruitful as we should – instead, we have invented new Gospels. Paul's presence in Jerusalem was necessary, he could not delegate this work to others – he was the seal of this fruit (the collection) of love.

All these congregations that had contributed were Paul's own, he was the one to present the delivery or gift to Jerusalem, to produce the effect he was concerned about, not merely to feed the hungry Christians.
- But the fellowship of the Gentile church with the centre – the bond, the wisdom, the gift of love.
- The Jewish Church in Jerusalem from which Christianity had come to the Gentiles. V30 – In all his plans, Paul put all his reliance on prayer (his own and that of the brethren for himself). This gift was a wonderful prayer to produce the bond among believers as a result of the gift of love.
- The gift was directed to God through Christ, through whom He sends His prayer – the medium of the Romans as well "their mutual or joint Lord" Jesus Christ, to whom they bow as Paul. And the love which the Spirit works in all believers' hearts, the love of intelligence. After delivering this "collection," Paul hoped to go to Rome "through God's will."
- A decision willed by God; and there, in the fellowship of the brethren was to be a safe, quiet haven to rest amid friends, in undisturbed fellowship – for this Paul's soul longed.

b) Paul sees the Roman congregation without trouble and harassment, like a lovely, quiet harbor; he sees himself storm-tossed and battling during that period ahead of him, he longed to reach home. The quiet haven, to drop anchor there for a while and come to rest, to reach this rest amid friends in undisturbed fellowship, this is what Paul's soul longed for. Paul did not at once proceed with his plans to come directly from Corinth to Rome, and he hoped that ministering to the saints would be "the last of the many things" that would cut him off from getting to Rome, but two additional years elapsed and then Paul arrived in Rome as a prisoner.

The congregation in Rome was truly endowed with all the spiritual gifts of a church and nowhere else do we find such an example.
- Paul had twice written to Corinth on a number of disturbing questions;
- He had written sharply to the Galatian churches, and here he tells us where to find the true fellowship of brethren. Rest, rest is his soul's longing, where there lay: unity, joy, peace and hope.

And with such a fellowship the God who in and through Christ has established this peace with us and fills our hearts with assurance and the joy of this peace – was indeed with Paul but much more Paul states; not for much longer would he have to stay in that sweet haven.
- The love of understanding imposed on him a duty.
- The duty of the Gospel in new areas.

Truly an amazing spiritual man!

c) The God of peace is the God who in and through Christ has established peace with us and fills our hearts with assurance and the joy of this Peace!

ROMANS CHAPTER 16:1-27
God's Wisdom (Firmness of the Heart)

This chapter is full of greetings and these greetings are a reference to unity, competency and fellowship with their resulting joy, peace and hope in the heart. Greetings break barriers and bring the people involved closer.

- Unity is not a result of being members of the same family or same tribe, it doesn't require riches or knowing the same things – all such external things do not bring about unity. The Scripture is the one and only place where we can draw the same things that bring about unity.

The Word is the one source of knowledge that brings about unity by changing man's heart through the power of grace in Jesus Christ our Lord.

Christianity never came into the world to make individuals highly intellectual just to stick out like the icebergs which float away in the wide sea in solitary terribleness; neither is it intended that we should be as anxious for our own Salvation as to be indifferent to the unity and welfare of others.

True religion is not a separating and repelling force, but rather, like attraction, it draws individual atoms into one body, and holds them together; it does not split into fragments, but welds into one; it is a loadstone, not a whirlwind (like a twister). God in His Grace gathers together in one body, all His scattered ones, and the same Spirit who compels us to love God leads us also to love our brethren.

As believers, we all come together as one – fulfilling the great plan of God's salvation which fills the hearts of men with the firmness in the heart. **When Paul saw this firmness of the brethren in Rome, his heart responded with praise and adoration. This was the experience of his heart – ever full of Christ**, the very depth of God's riches which he describes as **God's wisdom**. Any creature with a heart like Paul's could only fall down in praise and adoration – that He alone is wise, He alone is the fountain of all wisdom – all who have wisdom draw from Christ alone.

- This is the firmness of the heart.
- The infinity of God's wisdom is evidenced in the plan of salvation – for it is executed with absolute wisdom.

The Apostle's words, though they are venerable with years, as dropping heaven's dew upon all men, they are what should make believers praise also. Let nothing on earth distract us – we should feel the praise of our God like Paul did. Glory be to God who brings us to His salvation. Paul looks not only at the present but from the beginning to the end. God's Grace is set before us.

- This power of Grace is ours through Faith in Christ Jesus our Lord.
- His Office and His Person which are well presented in the previous Chapters. Christ has been made:
    1) Our Wisdom – unity, our great hope.
    2) Our Righteousness – peace on earth.
    3) Our Sanctification – joy on earth

    And these make us firm in the heart!

1) Our Wisdom - (unity, our great hope)

Christ is the true wisdom. This knowledge of Christ is wisdom. He is unto us Righteousness - this is **peace** unto us. Peace in our hearts. And peace is different from Joy. The joy is from Sanctification. This is the joy that fills the heart. This knowledge of God received by faith turns into wisdom because we have been reconciled to God when we received Christ as Savior. We need to see these things as Paul saw them here.
- Our faith - Christ in our heart.
- This is what happens when we received the Gospel of Christ.
- This Word in our heart is the Divine Power for our righteousness.
- His Blessed saving Doctrine.

Christ is the Word, by which He calls us to accept His work and His resurrection as our Salvation - the great hope.
- In such a manner, He received us by putting our faith and trust in him.
- Christ's acceptance of us sinners is pure Grace. He receives us irrespective of our sins. All believers should accept one another as a result of Christ having accepted us in grace. Here is a woman - Phoebe - a fellow believer. She should be received even as Christ has received you. In the same manner she had received many brethren and now she has brought the letter to the Romans.
- She had travelled over 2,000 miles to do business - so Paul sent her with the letter to the Romans. Paul says this woman is a fellow believer - she is to be received as Christ received you, her being a deaconess in Cencrea and having given reception to other Christians.

- Her reception of others was voluntary, she was therefore a minister who rendered help for the sake of help to those in need, especially the brethren. Christ received us – so we also should receive each other. Paul was the Apostle who lived by the obedience of faith in the publication of the Gospel and this obedience of faith with its gift of teaching, many were brought into the church. (Remember the church always means unity.)

On the other hand, we see this woman, with business acumen. Then we see the different groups within the Church membership in Rome known to Paul – having had their connection to faith as believers.
- The first group of these believers – those who met regularly at Priscilla and Aquila's home. These were Paul's fellow workers in Christ, a reference to their Gospel work in the Gentile Churches.
- Their work in Ephesus, the reception of each other, these had a Church and they laid down their lives for Paul's life. They had a Church at home for those who had moved to Ephesus with the first converts. Then Epenetus, Paul's first convert in Asia.
- Then Mary with her toil and devotion. Andronicus and Junias, who were converted before Paul. These are mentioned as the Jewish source of it's faith in Rome.
- Those with the source of the Gospel which had no error.
- Paul mentioned many other groups – all these eleven groups of people were personally known to him for faith's obedience. Another group which consisted of many slaves whom Paul had heard of because of this reception of each other was those of the House of Aristobulus and Narcissus – these were men of means in Rome who had come to faith.

- Then there were those of Imperial connection.
- Then Tryphena and Tryphosa – who had moved to Rome with their hard work in the Lord. They were two sisters.

These groups were all in various places in Rome. Paul wanted each one of them to salute the other – even as Paul sends his own salutation – they had to embrace each one with a kiss. The effect of God's righteousness is revealed in the unity; the acceptance of one another as a result of the gift of righteousness – the gift of grace which each one received by faith. This reception of each other is truly the wisdom of God.

2) Christ our Righteousness – (Peace on Earth)

- Yes there was unity among the Christians in Rome.
- Here are men perhaps who have never met each other but greet each other with a holy kiss. The salutation from Paul is to bind all the Romans together by being executed by the Romans as proxy for Paul – 9:12,16. In Paul's list, all the members of the Romans Church were included (representing Paul).
- They expressed the oneness in heart – this oneness bore this significance – mutual acceptance, penitence and reconciliation. In certain European countries they still offer and receive this public kiss. It expresses mutual forgiveness.
- A sign of the reconciliation that there is no barrier – but only the oneness which is manifested in the love of under-

standing coupled with purpose i.e. **based on the knowledge and result of God's work of Grace, the obedience of faith – Christ's righteousness – which comes from our faith with all that it involves:** mutual acceptance, public service and the gift of New Life.

This is the basis of a spiritual body – the acceptance of one another. For in the same way Christ accepted us – so must we accept each other. Then finally, salute you all the churches of Christ in Asia – yes Paul could speak for all these churches, apart from even these representatives who were with him at the time in Corinth.

This is the final salutation from Paul himself – Vs 25–27. Paul is with these other fellow believers, Timothy, Tertius, **Gaius** and those giving help – these are together with Paul and they all sent their salutations along with Phoebe. Phoebe is with the representative of the church in Corinth – sending their salutations to the Church in Rome – this is the spiritual body, the outcome of the righteousness they had also received from their faith by God's gift of grace.

- This is the righteousness that God puts in the hearts of His people who have faith. So when Paul looks to the vast knowledge of God – the greatest creature is only able to fall down in praise and adoration.
- For the creature sees that God alone is wise – for no one can be placed beside Christ.

All who have Christ's righteousness can only get this from Christ – there is no other plan of salvation which God could bring outside of Christ, even as there will be no wisdom outside of Christ. This knowledge brings us together in oneness and we accept this righteousness through the obedience of faith – for faith is the Power of Grace – which brings about the oneness among all believers.

Oneness is made up of Christ in our heart – the doctrine of the divine realities which reveals and teaches and admonishes.
- No earnest man should ever ignore the divine doctrine or realities.
- No man who is of sound mind can ever do without them.
- These divine realities include the Knowledge of Jesus Christ serving in obedience as a slave.

The Romans – the house of Aristobulus – there were many serving as slaves who knew well what being a slave meant.
- A slave cannot disobey; he/she must do as asked.
- Such a slave knows the Master, knows that his or her life depends on the Master.
- A slave would be the Master's greatest companion.

Many of the believers in Rome were slaves and so learned to obey their Master in a particular way – they knew what Christ did for them.
- We all know that in disobeying a worldly master you would be severely punished.

These slaves when they became Christians adhered absolutely to the teaching of the Apostles and so were faithful slaves. And they would take care of each other – their lives would never tolerate any other teaching which would result in disobeying the Master and cause break ups.

3) Sanctification – Joy on Earth

So Paul spent his entire life preaching the Doctrine of Faith. It was always Christ, and the trust in Him – the slave should always think of the Master and what He is to him. This Doctrine should eradicate all divisions and bring all to total unity. For this oneness holds permanently – the holding of all doctrine in totality – thus preventing all divisions – which is the firmness of the heart.

Christ, the doctrine has been thrown out of the hearts of many people today and thus they are riddled with disunity, discontentment and disagreement.

- These Roman Christians were vigilant in keeping the doctrine – hence the unity.
- All other doctrines separate – the wrong false doctrines separated the world. In the beginning – God saw the terrible sin in us who believed this false doctrine (ungodliness) – so sin came into the world and hence death.
- Today believers have no faith – no doctrine with many other activities replacing the truth (the doctrine of Christ) and so our world limps along with great difficulties; divisions, disputes, fights, enmity etc. In short there is no peace.
- The Christians of Rome always had in mind the Doctrine of faith (the Word).
- They were sound to the core – were immune to false doctrine.
- Christ is the true wisdom for all men, drop him and you are eternally condemned.
- But alas, many serve only the belly.
- No doctrine, no substance, no faith, no righteousness and no hope.

With faith in Christ, there goes our righteousness which is received through faith in Christ and this righteousness is our peace in Christ Jesus our Lord. Our righteousness is – adhering firmly to the doctrine. And this doctrine is the one we must preach to the rest of the world which is our sanctification to which we now turn.

- **Sanctification** – this is the teaching of the doctrine. With this teaching of truth we are enabled to see the same things of God from generation to generation as they all reach out in eternity.
- In all this period – the past, present and future, those who are one in the heart see the eternal power of God – His gift of Grace which stretches from eternity to eternity and in all the generations they are kept firm by the Power of Divine Grace.
- This firmness is the continued publication of God's Grace.
- The public heralding – from our souls and center – this heralding should be of Christ Jesus our Lord.
- We like the Romans should evermore be filled with Christ.
- This is what made the Romans firm – all these different groups knew one thing – what they had learnt – the Doctrine – and this they kept intact.
- This is the Gospel Paul preached everywhere he went.
- This is the only Gospel which was once found in the Old Testament.
- The Promise to Abraham – then the fulfillment which came to us in Christ.
- This was made known through the Apostles.
- Today we hear the prosperity Gospel, the new Gospel which is a counterfeit. The mention of only the title Christ and the miracles he can offer without the substance of grace. This is no Gospel at all.

- But the Gospel Paul preached was the same Gospel from Abraham which came down to the Apostles and to the Roman congregation.
- It should be the same Gospel we should hear even today.
- This is a revelation which has been made manifest in the Person and Work of Our Lord Jesus Christ.
- It began when Jesus sent the Apostles to the world.
- They carried the Old Testament, the Person and Work of Jesus.
- This is the publication which was made known to the Christians in Rome.
- What we see here in Rome is unity – yet what they heard (the Gospel) became Wisdom, Righteousness, Sanctification and Light (Life) to them.
- This is how we also become true slaves of Christ if we continue in the publication of the obedience of faith.
- In the obedience of heralding Christ alone, so that those who have not heard may hear and be made firm, even as the Church in Rome was made firm.

No wonder Paul exclaims, "To Him who has made you firm in accordance with the Gospel made public in accord with the mystery kept silent in eternal times, but made manifest by means of Prophetic writings, made known for faith obedience to all the Gentiles, to God alone wise, to whom, through Jesus Christ the glory shines to eternity. Amen."

If we read the Chapters together – we'd feel the unity of the Church, the firmness of heart which they all received in Christ alone. Faith received in Christ is the power of Grace. When faith starts to operate – this is Christ in our hearts. Faith is having Christ's work in our hearts. Paul calls faith the doctrine of all Churches.

- Christ in the hearts of all believers is the firmness which makes the Church grow.
- Embracing in our hearts the only true knowledge which comes from God is our wisdom (unity).
- Receiving one another as Christ received us is our righteousness.
- And continuing in the publication of the obedience of faith is our sanctification.

And these three are the ones that make our hearts firm.

The author

For the last thirty years, as well working as an accountant and setting up a successful Financial Systems Consultancy company first in Botswana and then in Uganda, Apollo Kikule has labored day and night in the study of God's Word, with particular reference and focus on the New Testament. In these studies, Kikule has found the spiritual truth to share with the world which comes from studying chapters in their entirety. He has found the congruence and uniformity in the meaning of each chapter and with all other chapters in the New Testament when read as a whole. The importance of individual writers i.e. the Apostles and Prophets disappears in thin air and what remains is the utterance of God; the inspired word. Within this utterance is the Law for conviction of sin and the Gospel with its gift of righteousness on contrition and faith for our salvation.

The author would like to thank his family, in particular his wife, niece and daughter for their constant and invaluable support.

Kikule's next two inspired books are coming soon:
The Acts of the Apostles and The Gospel According to St. Luke.

http://ancienttruthbyak.blogspot.com